THE REST
is up to you

by MATT SCHROEDER

Copyright

mattschroeder.org

Copyright 2012 by Matt Schroeder

The Rest is Up to YOU

ISBN-13:
978-1477461792

ISBN-10:
1477461795

Printed in the USA

Dedication & Acknowledgement

I want to give a special thank you and recognition to everyone who helped me throughout my recovery. This book has been an eight-year work in progress. Finally I am fulfilling my dream of helping other people help themselves through this inspirational writing. I would like to acknowledge Dr.Thomas E. Bauer, O.D. and other individuals not mentioned in the book who offered me support and encouragement.

Matt Schroeder

Life Turns on a Dime

Black ice. It had been raining for most of the day, December 6, 1997. I was traveling 35-40 miles per hour, significantly slower than the speed limit but obviously too fast for the road conditions at that time. You may have never seen black ice, and this is exactly why the invisible and slippery condition is dangerous; it can't be spotted, and it is extremely slippery.

Black ice is defined at Wikipedia: "Because it represents only a thin accumulation, black ice is highly transparent and thus difficult to see as compared with snow, frozen slush, or thicker ice layers. In addition, it often is interwoven with wet road, which is nearly identical in appearance. For this reason it is especially hazardous when driving or walking on affected surfaces." The definition isn't even as gripping as the real thing. And as my car twisted and turned inside out, upside down, and round and round, so did my life.

(Notes and life application before we move on with my accident: Just because we can't see something doesn't mean that it won't affect others or us. Many endeavors that we experience in life are much like an experience on black ice, and sometimes we can't see immediate results or effects; this doesn't mean that our

actions won't play a future role in our lives or the lives of others. Let's use a board game as an example in explaining this. When participating in a mind-stimulating game such as Scrabble (or any game that involves building off an opponent's plays) the words formed are contingent of where certain tiles were placed prior to our turn. The same is true in other facets of life too. Just because we cannot see the reason for something occurring doesn't mean it doesn't have one. As the lyrics, which the Byrds made popular in 1965, start out "to every thing there is a season," so too there is a reason for everything. Focus on the positive things in life at all times and know that God works in mysterious ways. Things will go smoothly enough as long as we stay relentlessly determined in our efforts to succeed. We won't be dealt what we cannot handle.

Whether it's my life or yours, many things can be made possible through dedication and persistence. I am a firm believer in that. Outside of humanly impossible tasks, for example, our bodies are not built for flight; most things that are presented in life can be tackled or defeated, leaped over or ducked under, or circumnavigated around. Usually talk about tackling, defeating, or beating gets associated with sports, but please do not relate these terms solely with winning or losing the match or game. That is unless you are referring to that competitor who never ever loses... you.)

Back to the accident: I don't remember the details of what all happened during that sudden car-spinning-on-black-ice tragedy. It came like a tornado and everything happened so suddenly. The memories and details are a blank in my mind. What I know of this incredible life-twirling accident that turned my world on a dime is only through the accounts of others. The accident account that I have heard about is from witnesses: fire fighters, rescue squad personnel, and family.

Dave Douglas, Columbus Grove, Ohio, volunteer firefighter, was the first to arrive on the scene of the accident. He could not determine what was human and what was car. He did not even know that the victim was a friend of his. Everything was twisted into a massive surreal blob of metal and flesh. The live wires posed a problem for the fire department, and the responders had to call Ohio Power to come out and turn the power off before they could attempt to pry the driver from the car.

Forty-five minute's response time was what the power company told the Columbus Grove Fire Department as there were lots of lines down in the area due to rain and ice. Dave was in shock at what he saw. Live wires were severed and extremely dangerous. The pole had split in half. The steering wheel was ripped off the car. The outcome did not appear bright as it did not look like the human, who appeared to be broken in half, would survive for forty-five minutes.

Keith Hartoon, another first-responder, risked his own life when he came to the car to rescue me before the power company could get to the accident and turn off the electricity. Keith was truly risking a lot because at home he had a wife and two beautiful daughters. Months later when I could thank him, I inquired why he went against code and helped while there were active power lines covering the car. His answer was that he could just feel that everything would be okay if he took the chance to help.

One of the Emergency Medical Squad crewmembers, Norm Schnipke, listened to my lungs on the trip to the emergency room; he wondered why he heard a gurgling sound in my lungs. It made perfect sense to him when he finally found out that my diaphragm was torn, and my stomach was jammed up into my lungs. Norm was very active in my church, and I knew him well. The emergency squad deserves credit for keeping me alive on the way to the hospital.

Once my beat up body was pulled from the wreckage, I was rushed to Saint Rita's hospital, in Lima, and my parents were called. Other than a small cut on my head, there was very little blood evident on the outside of my body, but internal bleeding was cause for much worry and uncertainty. I can only imagine the terror that was running through mom and dad's minds when they first saw me lying on the hospital bed. How empty, hopeless, and nearly dead my limp body must have appeared at the time my parents first saw me in a coma. I am the youngest of two children and their only son, which intensified the horror for them.

Solid Roots

My family - my parents and my sister Lisa - taken October, 2002. Don't I look studious wearing glasses? I need them only for reading now.

My family is a tightly knit group and has been for as long as I can remember. We took annual family trips when I was a kid to the Holiday Inn/Holidome in Ft. Wayne, Indiana where my family gathered and spent time together for a weekend. It was great. There were so many fun things to keep any youngster busy - from a pool, to an arcade, to putt-putt golf across from the lobby. Many fun times existed there as often times, one of my friends, a friend of my sister, or an aunt or uncle came with us.

Dad is one of nine children in his immediate family, and my mom is in the mix of five kids in hers, so our family is rather large. Growing up, I saw most of my aunts, uncles, and cousins weekly. Needless to say, my friends consisted largely of cousins. One of them, Mark, was my best friend when I was a little boy, and we were the same age but attended different schools. He grew up in Miller City, which is another small town in Putnam County about fifteen miles from where I grew up in Columbus Grove.

Summer vacations were a yearly occurrence in our family, and although we often went to theme parks, I was also included on more than one-or two-night trips several times. If you really enjoy eating at restaurants, then these trips were for you; I was one who really liked food. Sure, snacks, cold meat, fruit and veggies were always there for lunch, but most nights we typically enjoyed dinner at a nice sit-down place. By nice I mean any place to eat dinner away from home. That is my idea of vacation. Mom is a great cook, but there is something about restaurants' atmospheres that tickle my fancy. All-you-can eat buffets were definitely a treat when I was just with Dad, but Mom was not very keen on that idea. It made no difference to me because I just liked eating out. I was a very active boy so I needed food to keep me going and replenish the body.

(*For those of you who are blessed to have a close-knit family, be thankful and work on keeping it that way. Life goes a billion miles per minute these days, and it's so easy to let our priorities get out of whack. Whether you still live at home or near family, or thousands of miles away, make time to contact and connect with your family members. On the other hand, for those of you who don't have close family, you can still create close-knit ties that are like family to you. I know people who wouldn't call their family members "family" for many reasons, yet they have been able to develop wonderful relationships with friends who are closer than family. All the while, no matter how impossible it seems that your family will ever be like a real family, do your part to try and heal or create what can be a family with your family members. Then if they still don't respond or do their part, you will know that you have tried your best throughout life. Nothing is ever impossible. Remember that the word "impossible" can also read "I am possible." In other words, anything is possible. Be sure to visit my website http://mattschroeder.org for tips and suggestions on how to develop and nurture strong, healthy relationships.)*

I remember going on a family trip with the Kreinbrink's, relatives of ours, during summer vacation one year. Let me tell you, it was an adventure that will never be forgotten for a number of reasons My sister Lisa and I went with our parents early one sunny morning to meet at Uncle Tom and Aunt Joan's, and they took their daughter Judy. The Kreinbrink family had a full size van, so the seven of us had plenty of room to sit comfortably. We even had room for a couple weeks' worth of clothes. Although we had seven people, lots of clothes, and a big cooler, there was still room for one person to lie down, put his head on a pillow, and take a nap in the rear of the van while we were driving.

No one else on the trip was as young as I was, but it was still a neat experience. The Badlands, Mount Rushmore, and Crazy Horse Monument were our main destinations, but there were many stops made along the way. And as you can imagine, there were plenty of opportunities for one of my favorite things that put an exclamation point on vacation and that was FOOD! Our trip out west showed amazing scenery; friends and family were around me, and plenty of restaurants. What more could a person want?

The Badlands are just something you have to see to appreciate, and words cannot describe the miles of hills and rocks. The different colors in the rocks clearly make it one of the most attractive vacation sites I have ever been to. Mount Rushmore was also a magnificent site, and it was astonishing to see videos of how artists created the presidential portraits in the side of a mountain. It was done with such precision and the presidents' faces on the side of the mountain looked just like other photos I have seen of those presidents. The image was neater, in my opinion, at night, as the spotlights are strategically placed so the only things visible in the night sky were those carved-into-enormous-rock faces. The Crazy Horse Monument is much the same, being chiseled into the side of a mountain. It was interesting to see how both of these mountain sculptures were done.

All the attractions we saw were amazing, but oddly enough there is still another reason why that trip was so memorable. My Uncle Tom came down with serious sickness on the night we visited Mount Rushmore. I am certain Tom never walked to the beautiful sculpture carved into the side of a mountain as the other six of us did. Rather he stayed back at the van in the parking lot. It was quite odd to know we were out west at an historical monument, and Mr. Kreinbrink chose not to view it with his own eyes.

After the amazing night viewing of Mount Rushmore, we found our hotel and checked in. As soon as we became settled, Dad drove Tom to the hospital. There he stayed overnight! I am acquainted with hospitals now but back then they were foreign and frightening to me. That's why we younger generation people stayed in our sleeping corridors. I knew nothing about his situation except that Tom's burps smelled worse than raw sewage. And they were plentiful. He ended up spending the night over in the hospital. The next day Tom joined us as we continued our vacation. Luckily the problem was fixed, and the trip went on. The atrocious fragrance of gas exiting Tom's mouth remains burned in the memory of all in attendance. Those involved in this fiasco still joke about it today on occasion. He died about twenty years later in a tragic farming accident. There are many happenings to remember this family man by, and it is almost sad that one thing that sticks out and will be remembered eternally was an unfortunate health concern.

Another happy memory I have as a kid was dressing up for Halloween. At Grandma Schroeder's house, up in the attic, there was a costume and mask box that her grandkids would inevitably use at one time or another. Grandma joined us in Halloween fun every year. She liked dressing up and having people guess who was the person behind that mask. During Halloween we congregated at a relative's house and all the kids packed in a car, and a parent or grandma drove us around to other relatives in the area so we could trick-or-treat.

(Memories. Wonderful memories are in everyone's past. You may wonder why I bring up these maybe silly-but-fond memories. These are what make us who we are today, and they are also what make life so special. Good memories that stir up so much in you, even if sharing them with others who weren't there, seem silly, make up who you were, are, and will be. I challenge you to bring out some memories, even if it takes a while to find them and dig them up in the spider-webbed areas of your minds. Readers, I challenge you to find those great memories of your

past and wallow in them for a while. I know that some of you may not have had the memories you wish, but I can promise you that there are good ones. It is my challenge to you to find the good memories and hold on to them. It's not only healthy; it's crucial in order to move forward so that you can make choices to create more wonderful memories in your life now. Please email me with the moments that you want to share with others so that they can inspire other readers and viewers as I may share them on my website or blog. Email me: matt@mattschroeder.org)

Friends

Classmates: left to right, Clinton, Brian, Kurt, Ryan, Chad, me, Matt G. We gathered to celebrate my birthday as we typically did with one another. Mine worked out good for basketball that year. Would you want to get into a fight with that bunch?

A cozy brick house nestled in the country surrounded with woods on two sides near the village of Columbus Grove is where I call my home. Growing up, my neighbor friend Tony and I would spend countless hours in those woods, especially during the summer. We lived in a small neighborhood where everybody was a friend with one another. Columbus Grove was kind of like the television bar scene called "Cheers". It was a place "where everybody knows your name."

My adventures with Tony consisted of much more than swinging golf clubs, which we did. For crying out loud, we were young boys. It goes without saying that video games, outdoor adventures in the woods, sports, and digging in the mud consumed much of our time. Each fall we helped our neighbors gather and dispose of leaves that covered their yard like a blanket. Those neighbors lived through the woods that hovered near my house and across the road from where Tony's family lived. Tony and I spent many summer days kicking soccer balls, throwing footballs, and shooting hoops. My absolute favorite thing to do as a kid growing up was to practice basketball - rain, wind, or shine. I played basketball nearly everyday growing up. In my opinion, that made me one of the better basketball players in my grade school. Dad even put a light outside that shines on the basketball court at our house so we could play into the night. Basketball is my favorite sport, by far, and has been for as long as I can remember.

Tony and I liked to ride our bikes together, and many times we rode our bikes to Columbus Grove Swimming pool, only two minutes away and on the same country road where we lived. Whenever we went to the pool, we were instructed to wear sun block, and though we had every intention of doing that, we somehow occasionally managed to forget or wait too long to put on the block. Before we knew it, we wound up looking like a couple of lobsters. Our parents were the directors of the instruction behind the application of sunscreen, and they were obviously not exactly excited to see us transform into the shade of red. However, the concern was clearly out of love.

I remember when I was in about sixth grade and even younger, all my friends would have a little gatherings for their birthdays, and I also took part in this festive occasion. The congregation of friends was not like a birthday party with presents, but more like a social atmosphere. Having friends over was present enough, and when we went to someone's house, inevitably we would resort to a game of tackle football or basketball, whatever the weather made most suitable. I remember one year in May, when I had people over after school to celebrate the anniversary of my birth. Since it was the latter third of May, it was fairly warm. We had oodles of fun playing shirts versus skins in basketball.

Class gatherings were a big hit anytime of the year, not just on somebody's birthday. Often times it would be an overnight affair for me, but the one constant through all these celebrations was competition. I found anything that was a contest to be fuel for me and can remember some of these games like they were yesterday. I guess that explains how much fun they were to me. Tackle football was always a big hit at Brian Schroeder's (not a close relative) house. He had a large, tree-free, grassy area that couldn't have been a better layout for football unless Mother Nature grew a different shade of grass for boundaries and goal lines. Football games got pretty rough over there, and the rough nature of football carried through to basketball. Summertime was always good for a draining game of basketball, and when Brian's dad and uncle joined in it was more like barn ball. That is my term for a basketball contest that turns into a lot of rough housing. All of the fouling was done in a good-natured way, though. Nobody was ever determined to actually hurt anybody. Brian's dad and Uncle Mitch were bigger than anyone else. Whether my team won or lost was really insignificant, because we became tougher if nothing else.

I went with Brian's family to a family reunion type event at a hotel once. It was fun. His aunts and uncles reminded me a lot of mine, because they joked around a lot and kidded each other about everything. I had a lot of fun there and was introduced to the card game pinochle, but they called it Racehorse. The rules are slightly different than the traditional card game I've learned named pinochle but very similar, and it was so addicting that we played it until the early hours of the next day. I still play cards with that same group of guys at random times to this day.

When I said the card game was addicting, you have to understand that this particular game was new to me. When I try something new, I always want to learn and be successful at it. Cards are a big part of my life today, and anybody who is familiar with my family knows that trait is genetic. My dad is a huge card fanatic, and his mom was likewise until the day she passed away. My mom also enjoys playing cards, so it is practically a given that I play cards. On an average of once per week, I play Solo, which is an old German card game with rules and terminology not common to those of other card games. Most friends my age do not know, or care to learn, how to play Solo. So typically I find myself playing with those of the generation above me. I also play pinochle and double deck bid euchre.

Mark, my close friend as well as my cousin, and I went on annual, three day, two night summer camping trips with our dads. The trips were a lot of fun, and we always went to a Cincinnati Reds game during our second evening there. That was always preceded by a meal at Ponderosa. Mark always got a better bargain for his food than I did because he ate so much more than I. He was at the age when his stomach was like a bottomless pit. He was always very athletic. We brought gloves and a baseball to toss around at the campgrounds. Throwing football or Frisbee, riding bikes, hiking on trails, swimming, and cooking food while sitting around the campfire were all part of the state park experience. Every once in awhile we ran into a few snags but nothing our superhero dads could not fix.

One year we met at Grandma's house. Somehow when we left, my suitcase did not come along. When we unpacked at the park and realized that I had no clothes, we had to make a trip to the nearest store that had some clothes. The clothes were not of the same quality that we would have gotten at home, nor did we spend the same amount of time shopping for them. Both Mark and I were familiar with shopping with our moms. Most males are not into the thrill of shopping so the trip was short but adequate. This trip was not highly regarded, but the 45 minutes we spent to get my entire wardrobe still makes me laugh when I think about it. At home it would have taken us 45 minutes just to get a pair of jeans.

Some of our best times at the campgrounds happened while we rode bikes. The most fun was not usually on roads or campground loops but hiking trails in the wilderness. It was such a thrill speeding through the dirt paths that wound around through the trees. The best was when we passed through streams of water on our bikes, even through there was usually a detour route that avoided the water. Mark and I were both on mountain bikes so we did not mind getting a little wet and muddy. Besides, we were boys, and most boys like to get dirty while having fun. Some happenings will be left unsaid, even though we didn't do anything too bad or cause much trouble: the motto we went by is: what happens at camping, stays there.

(What were some of your past traditions? Do you still carry them on? Please fell free to share them with me via email matt@mattschroeder.org. I'll make sure to post some of these traditions at my website or Facebook page in the hopes that you'll get recognition for keeping tradition alive and to motivate others to start and/or keep time-honored customs and traditions. For those who didn't have any or many family and friends' activities that were repeated time and again, I encourage you to create some. This is especially addressed to those who are in relationships and to those who have children.)

Life is a Sport

Mark, with brother John and me, at one of our yearly Cincinnati camping trips.

All you had to do was give me a ball and basket to play with, and I could be content for hours. My cousins had a basketball hoop and playing area at their house, which was not as good as ours at home, but it kept me busy nonetheless. Dad and Tom, my mom's brother-in-law usually came out there with me for a while, and even Tom's daughter, Judy came out to play with me once in awhile. It was a rarity that she was not with my sister, but my sister Lisa was busy with her friends a lot and not always able to go with us over to the Kreinbrink home. Judy was busy doing things with her friends too, but she was usually home when we arrived in the early evening. Judy played basketball in high school so she could shoot decently. Tom and Joan also had a pool table in the basement but I rarely played billiards, and it was not much fun for me. When it became dark outside, I usually went inside to watch television because they did not have a bright light on their basketball court like we did at home.

If somebody delivered a Hollywood blockbuster about my life, the film would undoubtedly capture scenes of me shooting hoops at home or contributing to a school team in some way. Having a highly competitive nature is the best way to describe me. As a kid, my earliest memories are packed with games filled with chance and challenge. Whether it was a classic board game like Stratego, Risk, or Monopoly, or an active contest with friends or family members made no difference. The latter was most often the case as sports were typically played outdoors, and in the winter months a gymnasium was a place I could often be found. My father instilled being completive in me at a young age. My dad is still my biggest rival today. Competition drove me to make academic and athletic improvements in the early years of my life. The thrill of receiving the better score on a test or winning the game against friends and rivals, respectively, led to recognition, and I have always enjoyed being in the spotlight. What I have gained from the ways of competition continue to play a major role in my recovery efforts from a serious accident that took place in high school.

I have developed the practice of constantly putting forth a quality effort no matter what the situation or who the competition is. Attempting to better my Dad in anything gave me the greatest of all life lessons; try. My father never took it too easy on me when it came to athletics, and I was never able to reign supreme over him in any event. Without hesitation, I tried again. To me it always seemed conceivable to succeed in competition against him, but winning never became practical against Dad. After each defeat I rebounded with a positive outlook that it could be done the next time. My old man is and was an intelligent guy and most assuredly if my attitude turned negative after several failures, he would have let me win because, like most parents, he wanted his child to be happy. The try-again attribute would turn out to be priceless in my later life.

The academic portion of school was important to me as was athletics, but I practiced a lot more basketball than I did homework. Maybe that would bite me in the butt later in my life. I believe that in basketball it was always advantageous to be a better shot, and because more practice meant a better performance on game night, that was done. But a higher A did not improve one's GPA any more than a low A in our school, and just as my other family members (my cousins) all had a 4.0 GPA's, so did I. That is nothing for us to brag about because we just picked up on stuff easier. We were even taking Algebra I as eighth graders and later a calculus course as seniors for high school and college credit, concurrently. Math is the most important subject that if understood can enable you to meander through your other walks of life, to grasp and to solve problems in most subject areas. At least that's my take on it.

The all A-honor roll was always a goal of mine throughout school. Dad consistently rewarded me when I brought home my grade card at the end of each grading period. I was dedicated to doing well in school, but I seldom had many assignments to complete at home. I had the same amount of work as everyone else but, typically, my work got finished in my spare time at school so I could spend my hours at home doing fun things I enjoyed, like bike riding and playing basketball. My Dad was also a successful student when he was in school, and he helped me with any homework difficulties I encountered during school. He drove me to make academic and athletic improvements throughout my childhood and young adult life. The skills I've gained as a competitor in team sports continue to play a major role in my life today as I continue to adjust to life after having been in a major car accident that nearly killed me.

My eulogy could eventually begin by saying that Matt was always somewhat of a perfectionist who often times used victory as a mantra to live by. But hopefully nobody will need to worry about that until my life becomes complete. Nobody is perfect, and I surely have flaws, but that has never stopped me from trying to reach perfection. The desire to be the best I can be will help me make the most of this life.

(It is not so important what others think of you but what you think of you. If you find that you're challenging yourself enough, then excellent! If you find that you're not doing what is good enough for you, then listen to that little voice inside and do what is good enough and challenging for you. Live fully yet not foolishly and not by other peoples' pressures or expectations of you.)

Dad helped me practice for junior Olympics every year. He measured out the sprint and long jump distances, and then we would work on necessary techniques and skills for me to practice in order to do my best in those events. My Dad knows best, and that is the philosophy I used throughout most of my life. Whenever we raced in the backyard, my dad always crossed the finish line first, but I don't think he enjoyed beating me as much as he enjoyed watching me strive to improve so that I could keep up with him. My parents are and have always been extremely supportive of me. They were present and beaming with pride for me at every sports or school related event that I was part of. Win or lose, my parents were proud of me.

The Jaycees sponsored tri-skill events during both football and basketball seasons. Those were contests where the winners were recognized during halftime of the local high school sporting event. Tri-skill meant that there were three skills that judges would measure to determine a winner. In football they were the punt, pass, and kick skills. My Dad worked with me to improve my skill in these areas. The winner of the local event was allowed to participate in the district and then state levels. I remember one year when I was lucky enough to qualify for the state level. It was extremely snowy the day of the event. All the participants had the same snowy conditions to deal with, but I was not able to perform that well with the poor weather conditions. A joyous time it was competing in the punt, pass, and kick challenge, but when it passed, I turned my energy and focus toward basketball. At this point I was not yet involved in any organized team sports, but I was already foaming at the mouth, like a dog, to play basketball.

Thoughts of "That will be me someday" passed through my brain as I was watched the Columbus Grove Bulldogs compete in games during the 1985-86 season. Mom and Dad both enjoyed watching the hometown team take the court, and they had season tickets for all the home games. When I was only in the first grade, I went with my parents to several home games. I witnessed all the cheering and excitement surrounding the basketball games. Adrenaline floated in the air at the gymnasium, and Dad told me all about the rules and objectives of basketball. I told Mom, Dad, and my own self right then that I wanted to play basketball when I was old enough to get on an organized team.

I vividly remember going to the Elida Fieldhouse to see Columbus Grove play in the District finals against Wayne Trace after the 1985-86 season. Dad made it clear that the hometown Bulldogs had never been to the regional bracket, and that is where the winner of this game would go. Since that time my alma mater has played in the state championship game, but at the time it was the farthest Columbus Grove had ever been. The thrill of competition was high and my excitement was overflowing. The game was a nail biter, and the lead changed hands between the Wayne Trace Raiders and the Columbus Grove Bulldogs. Just before the game-ending horn, Grove missed an open shot that would have given my hometown its first regional berth. One of the best players on the team, Curt Darbyshire, missed a wide-open 15-foot jump shot that would have sealed the deal. It is amazing how that moment sticks in my head all these years. Curt is my friend now, and I often remind him of that moment today.

All year was basketball season to me, and I always had tri-skill in the back of my mind. Tri skill basketball consisted of dribbling, passing, and shooting, but the first two were relatively easy. Dad was the catalyst behind my basketball success. Although we had the proper lines and dimensions painted on our court, Dad would adjust the distances of the additional temporary lines each year. The shooting distances from the rim increased from year to year, and our temporary lines at home did too. The shooting was the only thing that I needed to work more on, and practice I did. As in the football competition, the top finishers were recognized at a high school basketball game. I was always one who liked the spotlight, so this was always a joy. With this recognition came the opportunity to participate in the district event, and the winner of the district competition received an entry for state.

I remember one year I made it to the state level in tri-skill basketball competition, and it was at Leipsic, which is only around 15 miles from home so we were there. I was elated, as my parents both were, on this day. Nervous was the feeling, but I welcome pressure. Big crowds of people do not bother me, and as mentioned before, I enjoy being in the limelight. As some prognosticators would say, I had ice water in my veins. Near the end of the competition, I was in the lead, and we were just waiting for this one competitor, who could still beat me with a great score in the shooting competition. I was on pins and needles waiting for him to shoot. There is no greater feeling of anticipation than the events over which you have no control, I feel. My opponent hit almost all his shots, winning the competition. But that loss was one that was good for me. I was never in that same situation again, but it prepared me to make the best of the unexpected and unwanted outcomes that are inevitable in life.

Larry Bird and Me

Me at age 17, Dad at age 47, and we're still horsing around...

I have great admiration for Larry Bird. I have studied his life by reading books and articles about him and by watching his basketball career closely. I have attempted to emulate the greatness that I see in Larry Bird on the basketball court. Granted I was not blessed with the height or skills that Larry Bird displays, but I believe we share a few of the same characteristics. As a kid, before my accident, I practiced basketball constantly. Shooting hoops at my house was a regular habit. Like Larry, the rain didn't stop me.

I had his first book, <u>Drive</u>, I collected as many facts and articles I could find on him including "Sports Illustrated" covers, and eventually I had his second autobiography, <u>Bird Watching</u>. I even have two biographies written on Larry Legend by other authors. I have several "Sports Illustrated" magazines that are framed and hanging in my room, featuring Bird on the cover, but they are from his professional career. The only "Sports Illustrated" magazine that would complete my Bird collection would be the one where he was playing for Indiana State.

I have lodged at a place formerly known as "The Larry Bird Boston Connection," in Terre Haute, Indiana. Indiana State, Larry's alma mater is located in that city. It was during a summer vacation when my parents brought me to Frenchlick, which is where Larry grew up, and he also built a summer home there. We drove around the little village that was not much to look at. The one nice home there was Larry Bird's, and the information I was reading in the backseat said that he spent some summers there. The Bird residence was practically a mansion that sat far away from the road with a full court basketball-playing surface in front. It sat on a very large piece of land. It truly was a flowering plant in a garden full of weeds, as his neighbor's houses looked very haphazardly taken care of.

The closest I have gotten to meeting Larry Bird, or his wife rather, was when I spotted his wife jogging in Frenchlick. I was so excited to see her and possibly have the chance to meet her that I tried to talk to her, but not to my surprise, I was denied. Dad did not want to bother her workout routine. One day I hope to meet Larry Bird, but for now the autographed pictures will suffice.

Many times when Dad would play basketball with me because I had no older brothers and my sister was not interested in playing hoops, quite frequently we would pretend that we were Mr. Bird or some other basketball great. Dad taught me to play a game called 21, and I rarely, if ever, beat him. I tried my best to beat my Dad at anything and everything we did and always seemed to come up short of victory. But I constantly reminded myself that there would always be "the next game" and perhaps another opportunity to win right around the corner, and if not an opportunity to win then at least an opportunity to practice and improve my skills. It is that practice of trying again that is pivotal to experiencing success in any walk of life.

(I want to stress the final sentence of that paragraph to you. "It is that practice of trying again that is pivotal to experiencing success in any walk of life."

How has something prepared you for the unexpected and unwanted outcomes in life? Perhaps you have been lucky enough to avoid unfortunate happenings, but it seems inevitable that life throws everybody random curveballs. Although we cannot predict catastrophic events accurately, there are ways that we can use our own experiences to cope with what happened and get ready if something were to happen. I used faith and family to prepare myself for what happened, and the same was used after bad experiences to deal with circumstances. I am asking you to reflect on your life, skills, and/or relationships, and please develop a personal plan of dealing with catastrophe. Everyone is unique, so are their happenings, and there is no right or wrong answer.)

My Coach

Dad was not only a literal coach for many different sports before high school but also my personal coach throughout everything else that comprises my life. Mom told me when I was younger to try and be like him, and I lunged at the idea. We still make constant competitions and joke around with everything. I took Mom's advice to heart: Dad means the world to me!

With all this talk about sports idols and other people we admire, another person was and still is my ultimate hero - my dad. Because of my hero who was also my assistant coach, my eighth grade basketball season was possibly my most memorable season.

I went to a small Catholic school, and all of the boys in my class were on the team. We beat some decent teams that year and finished second place in the tournament we were in. I was not the fastest player on court in junior high or high school, but I had quick hands and knew where everyone was at on the floor. If smart ball is played, an illusion makes it seem like a player is quicker than they really are. My understanding of the nuances of the game is credited to my father.

Saint Anthony's, where I went to grade school, first started a junior high track and field team when I attended. Because the program was just starting to flourish, it was not very powerful. The enrollment numbers were not very large and maybe that was a more significant reason why the track team was not very good. Nonetheless I am proud to say that I was a part of the team. When I was younger, sprinting was my strong suit, but as several years passed, I was not quite the sprinter that I once was. I ran the 400-meter and the 200-meter runs. I am a purebred competitor, and I did not easily accept finishing in the middle of the pack. I was not that good at track, but I learned to view each race as a challenge to improve my personal best time. I participated in track for only one season. I love sports but track is one that I never miss.

My Dad was awesome when it came to helping me develop skills for whatever activity I was participating in at the time. Before it was time to start playing organized tee ball, my Dad built me a tee. This was not a run of the mill tee that could be bought in a store. This tee was much better. The half inch wide steel pipe, jutting from a solid wood base, had a four-inch rubber shock absorber near the tip, and it was used for hours of playtime. After tee ball came peewee ball. Dad was my coach for tee ball and peewee ball. He put up a curved fence backstop for me when I was learning to swing the bat. Nobody is perfect, and the backstop would help with any ball I whiffed at. I had fun with Dad always, and some things never change.

Little League came after peewee, and Dad was no longer my coach but he was always willing to help in anyway he could. We went to the batting cage whenever he helped me with my hitting, because I could now hit the house from the backstop or even worse hit my Dad. Dad even worked with me on fielding. I never played the outfield in game situations, because I was better at playing infield.

I remember my first time playing A-squad when I was the youngest player on my team. At the plate my performance was not something to write home about, but I excelled at fielding the ball. This again is something my Dad helped me with. I recall fielding practice on uneven turf at home with him. Kids who were two grades above me in school were my teammates that year. Hitting against other school's team's pitchers was not my strong point the first year of little league, but I never let that get me down, and Dad never stopped working with me to improve in that area. The coach, however, used my fielding as an example when showing others the proper mechanics of how to play infield. I was sound when it came to knowing how to position my body when a grounder was coming because Dad brought home different fundamental tips tapes from the library. I improved significantly from the plate in my remaining little league time.

There was still one more step before high school ball and it was called Pony league. There were enough boys in Columbus Grove playing baseball when I was in seventh grade to field two teams. Players were not assigned to either team based on skill level. It was supposed to be random, but it was basically a group of friends versus another group. Most of the boys that went to the parochial school were on one team, and the boys from public school were on the other. There were a few exceptions, but generally, separation by school was the case. The season was about over and the big showdown between the two rival teams from the same town was up next on the schedule. There was a minor issue with the date of the game which had been postponed due to rain. The make-up game was to be played in the late afternoon on the day Larry Vennekotter and his two boys returned with Dad and me from our annual three-day Cincinnati Reds fueled camping excursion.

Family always came first though, and we didn't let the Pony League game impact our trip too much, but I was careful and made sure that I was not ailing after our campground adventures. It was a good thing I wore my jersey on the journey northward, because we went straight to and arrived at the game less than 30 minute prior to its start. I was pitching, and heightened pressure by the attendance of the person who I had the greatest desire to impress, my cousin Mark, only allowed my best performance of the year. My team was easily victorious, and the best part was the opponents were our classmates.

I was not overpowering as far as speed goes, but I used a repertoire of pitches. My signature pitch was the curveball, and it was great to have Uncle Larry there to see it since he taught me how to throw it. The most memorable part of that game was striking out Nate Schaublin three times, with a curveball every time. He was a friend who happened to be one of, if not the best, power hitter in the area, but a breaking ball he had not mastered yet. Those strikeouts were maybe even more rewarding with Mark there to see that outing.

(The steps in your life prepare you for your future. What steps, whether in sports, hobbies, school, or other areas prepared you for life? What steps are you taking now to create a balanced present and a successful future? Think about the things you are thinking, saying, and doing that are creating who you are now and who you will be tomorrow.)

Rivalry and Competition

Me, approximately six years of age, wearing medals from Junior Olympics. I am standing in our backyard where Dad practiced with me for running and jumping events.

As a kid I spent many afternoons at the pool and learned a variety tricks from watching the older kids flip off the board in wild directions. After carefully watching their movements I soon began bravely attempting the same tricks off the board. And after several failures including belly flops and hard smacks to the water, success followed. When I saw somebody do something that I thought I'd like to do, I mimicked their movements off the board to the best of my ability. Like mathematics is best learned by seeing examples and then attempting similar tasks on your own, at least that's what worked for me, so too new tasks are mastered. Flips and dives, back flips and dives, and a series of twists were all part of my diving repertoire off the springboard. I may not have perfected my specialty dives, but they were always good enough for me.

My misfortune with injuries started in my early adolescent days at the swimming pool. It sounds rather illogical to come into injury while partaking in the so-called relaxing water activity yet "anything but calm" can be used to describe my behavior when it involved sports or physical activity. I took my diving board skills, after I had become good at them, over to the wall of the seven foot deep section. My platform there was a concrete platform instead of a springboard and successful maneuvers were completed many times. When a person is least expecting it is when accidents seem to happen. Stitches were needed after splitting my head open.

The front portion of woods about one quarter of a mile away from our house was loaded with raspberries one year and my competitive nature only helped my love of eating. It sounds strange to mention competing when speaking of picking berries, but it is true. You see there was another man picking, and even though there were plenty of raspberries to go around, I felt threatened. I wanted to pick all the berries for they were good, but clearly that would not happen anymore. It was man against boy! This was an old man, and he looked like an experienced raspberry gatherer. Riding my bicycle back and forth between the woods and house took, what I thought to be too much time, because this mysterious guy had his truck parked right alongside the road. Scratches and scrapes from the thorny patch mattered not to me because the tasty reward was well worth it. This experienced man was prepared. He had gloves that went up to his elbows to protect his arms from the scraping bushes. He had a bucket fastened around his neck to free both arms for gathering the mouth-watering fruits. He may have been better prepared and had me in age and wisdom, but I was up to the challenge. Weary is how my legs felt after a day full of collecting fruit but a rejuvenating night's sleep, after a bowl of vanilla ice cream topped with fresh berries, got me ready to attack the next day with ferocious abandon.

(Competing against yourself is the fiercest but most beneficial battle one can face. At least that's what I have come to realize. A personal challenge is what needs to be done. You have the ability to set high goals for yourself, as long as they are realistic and attainable, and striving towards and reaching them is the ultimate reward. As the Egyptian pyramids weren't built in a day, so high goals don't need to be achieved in the first attempt but broken down into smaller ones. Trials, errors or failures, and new attempts, which may be followed by more repetitions, might need to be done at each level. The smaller goals need to be easily attainable yet increasing in difficulty at each level, because that way you can experience success constantly.)

Rivalry and competition can keep you working hard and striving continuously to improve. Speaking of rivals, my friend Mark Vennekotter was probably my biggest rival, away from home when I was an adolescent. I list him as a rival not because our teams faced each other often, but it seemed like we were always in competition with each other because of our closeness in age. The competition between us started when we were very little by our sisters being proud and trying to make their brother sound better than the other, but it continued between Mark and me as we began organized sports.

Before and during the season I worked on baseball at home with Dad but occasionally, Lisa helped. My older sister loved to see her little brother do well at sports, and I could find her in the stands from time to time. She would occasionally throw baseball with me. Usually she would get disgusted with me and threaten to stop playing catch and go in the house if I threw one more with too much velocity. It was hard not to throw a quick one randomly because I tossed back and forth with Dad, Mark, or a teammate most often.

When I reached Pony League, I was a pitcher. Mark was an all-star-caliber pitcher. We were best friends who always looked forward to high school where we figured to meet often. We would always jokingly trash talk to each other about what would happen when we met, and we rooted for each other whenever possible

After what seemed like an eternity, Mark and I would finally meet on the baseball diamond during the summer before high school began. Columbus Grove would host Miller City. Although Miller City is in Putnam County, we did not play them in the regular season. Since Mark was regarded as a great pitcher in the area, I was anxious to play his team in hopes that he would be pitching. For several contests that year he was occasionally still helping his classmates on Pony League, but Mark had been upgraded to the Acme team (which is summer baseball for those slated to be sophomores through seniors in high school that fall), so our long awaited head-to-head confrontation was no longer a certainty.

(The sport my Grandma Schroeder referred to as simply "ball" (baseball) falls under lesser importance when comparing it with life happenings. For most people, my experience that summer can be a learning experience. If there are unforeseen circumstances that arise out of nowhere, such as meeting Mark and the rest of his classmates seemed inevitable when the schedule came out, but suddenly was in doubt, please just roll with the punches and make the best you can out of every situation. Maybe you made a critical error at work that will cost you, the company, or your boss dearly. It's not the time to cry over spilled milk or act like you're up the creek without a paddle, but rather do what you can with what you have.)

I had no worries except trying to determine how to win the next game, and if facing Mark would happen now or not. I didn't have to wait for another time to face Mark, because when their bus pulled in, I saw him meander to their dugout. As soon as we had their book, sure enough, we saw that Mark had a "1" in front of his name, which meant he was pitching. We were friendly rivals finally getting a chance to meet.

I was playing shortstop and did not have to worry about taking the loss on the mound. The Miller City team was good enough without Mark playing, but they were excellent with him. Mark struck out almost all the guys on my team at least once. He tried to punch me out on strikes, but I was not about to let my arch-rival (and cousin) strike me out. To strike out against Mark, either swinging or looking, would be detrimental to my self-esteem when we saw each other next. I reached first base on a powerful ground ball that shot between the opposing second baseman's legs. I stole second base and was in scoring position with no outs. I came around to score our only run of the game. Granted it was unearned, but a run nonetheless. We may have lost the game, but it felt like I won the battle between Mark and me. We spoke afterwards, and I congratulated him on the fine game he threw. He acknowledged with a slight twinge of disgust saying that he knew that I would not get out on strikes. We were looking forward to our future head-to-head contests.

Hindsight is 20/20, and I have learned that competition is about much more than just winning the game. The value of the game is more about camaraderie than anything! However, I did not see this while I was playing sports as a youngster. When I was a kid I associated not getting a higher or better score with failure and losing. This is much different than my view today. Today, as an adult who has experienced win and loss and things out of my control, I realize that it is most important to have fun, to practice and improve on one's skills, and to not only be the best I can be, but to help others be great too. Teamwork comes into play big time in team sports.

All of the hype between Mark and me had us looking forward to our high school contests in basketball and baseball. Mark's team was the Wildcats, and I was on the team called the Bulldogs. When we were sophomores Mark made varsity basketball and I was on the junior varsity team, so we would not face one another on the court until later. I looked forward to the Miller City basketball game my junior year because Mark and I were sure to finally meet on the court since I was playing Varsity that year. But since we played Leipsic before the Wildcats and I wound up tearing my ACL, I never did get the chance to play Mark on the court that year. Our last hope of facing each other in high school sports would be our senior year when I would hopefully be back on the court after rehabilitating my ACL.

When my senior year arrived and my knee was not quite up to par for the high school basketball team, I had an interesting decision to make. After discussion with the varsity coach, we decided that I would start the season playing CYO (Catholic Youth Organization) ball, and after Christmas I would come back to the high school varsity because they needed a shooter. Even though I was no longer one of the quickest players, I had continued shooting, and maybe had even improved in that aspect of the game.

Having Mark as a rival obviously played a role in recovery from my knee mishap, but maybe my desire to return to a normal life after my knee reconstruction held an equal if not greater importance. High school was getting close to done, and I wanted to enjoy it as well, like everybody should. Many experiences and memories were had with classmates. Much college preparation, filling out scholarship applications and taking college preparatory classes was done in order to have a smoother transition into post high school life. I knew high school was only a small piece of the pie called Life.

Having it All Planned Out
(Or so I thought)

Young Matt ready to hit a home run.

My friends Clinton, Kurt, and I had our lives all planned out. We were going to follow in Clint's two older bothers' footsteps, and attend The Ohio State University in Lima for one year before heading to Columbus to major in mechanical engineering. We had intentions of rooming together in a rental house when we got to Columbus. We even took a day off school to go on a college visit the year before. It was a mini vacation masked as a college visit because we were set on Ohio State for college. It was just a day to get out of school, as many college visit trips are, and we had a blast soaking up the college environment.

Everything was going very well as I worked toward wrapping up my senior year of high school. I earned good grades and had a college plan set in place, and I had determination to persevere through rehab for my torn ACL. I truly aspired to make a difference on the court of the game I love, basketball. If my surroundings and happenings in high school could be referred to as branches, I felt I had the whole tree in my hands. This is until the day the tree was completely uprooted, lifted, and splintered into a million pieces as if in a tornado. My life plans had been shattered even more so than the twisted human-and-metal I had suddenly become.

Until...

Life Has its Own Game Plans

December 6, 1997, the day of the big game that I had been waiting for, our first scheduled CYO game, was right around the corner. I was really looking forward to getting back to organized ball after about ten months of rehabilitation on my injured knee. I wore a bulky cti^2 brace on my knee when I played basketball. The brace was something I became used to because I knew it was necessary for me to wear it in order for me to prevent any further knee injury. I wore it without complaints because all I wanted was to play basketball. I loved pushing myself and practicing and improving my game every step of the way

Saturday morning, the day before the game I had been hyping myself up for; I went shopping with mom to buy a new winter coat. Most people would be excited about buying new winter apparel, but I was too preoccupied with anticipation and excitement for the first CYO basketball game of the season and my career. I recall specifics relating to that shopping adventure and shopping at J.C. Penny in the Lima mall. That baffles me as shopping was not my forte.

There was a Columbus Grove girl's basketball game that afternoon, December 6. At some point I had to leave the gym before the game was complete and go to work at The Pizzeria. I do not remember what team my hometown team was doing battle against, but I can tell you that I was indeed there. It was a routine occurrence for me to attend any Columbus Grove sports event when I had a little spare time. I liked going to all the basketball games that I could. Even today, I remain an ultimate fan of Columbus Grove High School teams.

Chad Ricker, who was my boss at the highly acclaimed local pizza restaurant, was also at the game but left much earlier since he had to open the store. I say "highly acclaimed" because in Columbus Grove, it was the popular high school hangout or gathering place after football and basketball games. Chad became one of my better friends through the years. We all used to have a lot of fun at work. Pulling pranks on each other was a regular occurrence.

A great background, supportive family and friends, successful basketball and athletic record, and college plans in place - yet nothing prepared me for what life was about to slam my way.

I do not remember the moments that led up to when I lost control of my car. I was delivering pizza dough to another Pizzeria a few miles away. I do not recall the instant my car smashed into a utility pole, changing my life forever.   People tell me that it is better that I don't remember the terrifying moments from my accidents, but at some point I wanted nothing more than to remember the precise details of the accident.

Luckily the only passengers in my car were two buckets and two trays of pizza dough; no other cars were involved.   The battle was between me and a utility pole. If there were judges, I would undoubtedly be declared the winner, but there were none. I drove my car onto the black ice and lost control of my car, spun around, and smashed my driver's side door into a utility pole. The transformer, knocked loose from the pole, came crashing down on the car and me, and the electrical power lines toppled onto the car as well.

The live wires were severed and quite dangerous. The pole had split in half. The steering heel was ripped off the car. And, I was nearly broken in half. I broke my femur, the thigh bone, completely in half, and a metal rod, which will never come out, had to be inserted in my left leg. There is long scar on my left hip from where the rod was inserted. My pelvis was shattered in pieces and would need time to mend. An incision mark down the back of my neck is a permanent reminder of the two broken vertebrae in my neck that were fused together. A scar, from being cut open to pull my stomach back down to where it was supposed to be, runs from the middle of my chest to my waistline. Though it was a successful tummy placement, my belly still sticks out a little after I eat; at least I like to blame it on the surgery. After I was stitched up, doctors had to reopen my belly, because it got infected during the healing process. Luckily I have no recollection of this, but I have proof. There is an ugly, two-inch wide scar down my chest. Initially, I tried to conceal the lengthy scar by wearing a shirt all the time, even when I swam, but I have learned not to be scared of letting others see my scars. The minor injuries included several broken ribs. Last but definitely not least, I had a traumatic brain injury (TBI). Whether the TBI is a result of the transformer hitting my head, or if there was something else that happened, the brain injury is what slightly affects me today. Because of TBI, my speech delivery is slightly slower and my reaction time is supposedly slower.

This sudden onslaught on my life called "a car accident" was an occasion different than practicing basketball because there was no way to improve on it the next time or insure that it won't happen again. This would prove to be hard for me to accept, extremely difficult to accept, to say the least.

Live or Die?

My Ford Taurus, taken December 7, 1997. I have always driven a Taurus and continue to drive one today. After surviving this wreckage, I feel the Ford Taurus is a safe car.

The first night in the hospital I was in very bad shape and an initial prognosis was that I could pass away at any time. At one point, I even coded and was nearly lifeless. My parents did the best thing they knew to do for me while I lay helplessly in the hospital room: they prayed for me. Mom, Dad, and my sister stayed in a family room of the Intensive Care Unit (ICU) at St.

Rita's that first night. My parents stayed the whole time that I was in Lima, but my sister Lisa went home to get supplies and to work as a nurse's aide at a local nursing home. My parents ate, showered, and slept at the hospital for several weeks. I still feel like I am indebted to them for the rest of my life or theirs, whenever God decides to take us from earth.

Doctors put me on a rotating bed so pneumonia would not develop in my lungs. I have been told that the bed made no sudden movements, but was in a very slow and constant state of motion. It was supposed to stimulate my brain. Mom recounted that she hated to see me rotating in that bed. She agrees that it was the best protocol, but she still did not like to see her baby like that. Both parents agreed that I looked huge lying there. My cardiovascular activity was at a standstill. I was relatively physically fit, but I appeared larger than normal because my body was swollen from surgery procedures and injuries from the accident.

Doctor O'Rorick had just come to Lima recently from another Ohio based trauma center, and I was fortunate that he was there to perform my surgery. I like to think that he was the neurosurgeon who saved my life. I personally know a nurse who has since told me, and Mom also informed me, that a lot of people at the hospital thought that Doctor O'Rorick was wasting his time and effort in my scenario. At first there was not much skepticism, but after the first couple emergency surgeries, with no signs of drastic improvement, things seemed dim. Jan Barkimer, a friend from Columbus Grove and Saint Anthony's parish, was my main nurse when she was on the clock in the Intensive Care Unit at Saint Rita's. Even she expressed that while I was in the hospital in

Lima after my accident occurred, the prospect of me ever living a productive life was not looking very optimistic.

My parents were informed that the chances of my recovery and ever leading a productive life again, much less even coming out of the coma, were slim, but they never stopped hoping and praying for a successful recovery. I believe that prayer is the best medicine for people in the condition I was at the time - fighting for my life. When working with people, in dire circumstances or not, when direct help is not possible, it is best you do what everybody has ability to do, and that is to pray and to hope. Prayer has always played a regular role in my life and also in my family and most of my friends' lives. Most of my friends were raised Catholic. Going to the parochial grade school only intensified my religious upbringing. Dad and Mom had the greatest influence on my life though, and all other influences in my life only added to my spirituality. Father Keith McCormack had been the priest at the grade school I had attended since first grade, at Saint Anthony's. While I was staying at the hospital, he gave me the last rites two times. This blessing is called the anointing of the sick now, but it is usually given to people just before they die. This is how close to death I was at the time after my accident.

I really feel bad about what my parents went through after I was in that accident, although it was clear that the accident was beyond my control. My heroes stayed by my bedside day and night, offering prayers and attempting to help me return to normalcy. While I was yet in a coma, they would massage hands, arms, and feet, and move my arms for me. My neck could not be massaged because I had a Miami J collar on. The collar was needed since two vertebrae were broken and fused together in my neck. I guess people only really worked with my right arm because

51

there was a blood clot in my left arm that limited how much it could be manipulated.

While I was not conscious for the care and attention my parents, the nurses, and the doctors had given me, monitors tracking my heart rate indicated an increase when Mom or Dad talked directly to me. Whether I actually heard them or not is unknown, and doctors insisted that it was a natural response, but those monitors gave my parents hope that I would eventually come out of the coma. I truly believe that, subconsciously, I heard the people around me who were bringing comfort to the situation. Dad even played catch with me while I lay in the hospital bed. As I was lying in the bed, lifeless, Dad would put the ball in my hands, and I would throw. Doctors did not want to give Dad false hope, and they told him it was an involuntary action, a reflex, of the body. We may never know whether the years of playing sports and throwing ball made any difference or not, but it helped to create a positive atmosphere with family and friends.

I would lie there appearing non-responsive when people talked to me, but when family or friends spoke, the heart rate monitor increased. Mom and dad spent hours on end talking to me, and I wish I could have shared conversation with them. Many different tactics were used to try and bring me out of the coma. Uncle Karl came to the hospital and brought a hometown pizza with him. It was a nice gesture for my parents, and they even decided to attempt waking me from unconsciousness with it. The pizza smell was wafted my way, but it did not wake me up. I am surprised that I never woke up because I loved Pizzeria pizza. If food couldn't get me up and moving, would anything ever make that happen?

After 21 days I was still in a coma but had stabilized enough that doctors determined it would be best if they moved me from ICU to a facility that would accept a patient in my level of coma. Many places would not take me as I was unresponsive to anything. Dodd Hall at the Ohio State University medical facility in Columbus willingly accepted me as they specialize in brain and spinal chord trauma patients. The University has since been critically acclaimed for their stem cell research and their helping patients recover from serious trauma and or paralysis.

Dad and Mom, for the first time in a month, spent most nights at home, because the family was not permitted to stay at Dodd. My hometown, Columbus Grove, despite sharing its name, is nowhere near Columbus. It was nearly a two-hour trek just to go to Columbus from our house, but the distance would not keep my family from showing their support for me. Mom and Dad each took two weekdays and on Wednesdays, Lisa would come to Columbus. For seven plus weeks in Columbus I was still comatose, and certainly the time there with me was not that enjoyable. So many times one of Dad's siblings would come to keep my family member company because one-way conversation got old fast.

Typically family members stayed until 9:30 p.m. during the week. This allowed them to get home at a relatively decent time since they had to go to work the next day. Their places of employment allowed them to reshuffle their schedules so a full time status could be maintained. Their employers were flexible, given the situation. The weekends when both parents and my sister would come, they stayed in a hotel on Saturday night.

On one particular visit my mom brought along Aunt Teresa to keep her company, as carrying on a conversation with me was impossible, and it turned out to be a difficult day to cope with the

53

situation. On this day Mom was informed about my prognosis. She hung onto hopes of recovery, but hearing my prognosis dulled her spirits temporarily. Doctors informed her that when the coma ended, I would need to live in a nursing home because I would be unable to walk or care for myself. By this thinking, I would more or less be a vegetable. She could not bear seeing me lie there and although she had hope, the "experts" tried to tell her otherwise. The reports of the day left Mom struggling to watch me, so she headed for home. Luckily, Teresa was there for Mom to confide in and help her get home safely. Many things were running through Mom's head.

She prayed that I would make a miraculous recovery, and also that I if I did not make some kind of extraordinary recovery, that I would die peacefully. That sounds a bit morbid, but I assure you that it isn't. She knows now and knew then that I have an active spirit. Being confined to living in a nursing home at such a young age, unable to care for myself, would be devastating. I agree with my mom's thoughts. She always only wanted me to be happy, and she thought that I would not be unless I made some recovery. My parents were given only the tiniest bit of hope, but luckily they remained positive.

While I was in a coma for more than ten weeks, many visitors came to see me and offered support for my family. Family, friends, and coworkers came to visit. I could only begin to let you know who all came at both Lima Saint Rita's and Dodd Hall in Columbus for Mom kept a journal when I was out of commission, but it is probably unreliable to depend rely on her notes, because surely people were forgotten.

Prayers were the most powerful prescription that doctors could not order. Prayers came from all over the United States. I was put on nationwide prayer chains. If prayers could be taken from a bottle of pills, I would want an indefinite number of refills. If the situation looked gloomy, you could pop a pill. I do not know how much a bottle would cost but prayer is free. Prayer is always a conceivable action because the price is always affordable in this money-crazed world.

In fact, while I was in the hospital, before every CYO basketball game, the team I was going to play for (before my accident) and whoever the opposing team was each game, the coaches, and the officials joined at half court in a moment of prayer for me. Before the accident occurred, I was strong in my faith and afterwards, I feel even stronger about my faith.

(I must add that personal beliefs belong to an individual. I am not trying to influence your thinking. I was raised Roman Catholic but I understand that we all have a choice to follow and believe what we would like. I don't feel like I am better than anyone for believing the Roman Catholic faith. While this is where I put my faith, I don't expect the same of everyone else.

I wholeheartedly believe that every person should have fun during their lifetime but also that the individual doesn't need to reap rewards to exemplify the fun had. People often see having fun as a "what's in it for me" factor. When others who may be less-fortunate people, are able to experience a certain happiness as a result of your actions, that will give you great joy and fulfill that fun factor I was speaking of. I'm talking about charity. Before you get all upset, please note that I am not suggesting neither monetary nor material gifts but merely saying that giving should not be about receiving things in return. Charity is ultimately about going the extra mile (hypothetically speaking) and doing altruistic things so others' can put themselves in situations that promote their lives to be better.

"If you give a man a fish he'll eat for a day, but if you teach him to fish, he'll eat for a lifetime." In other words handouts

are not the answer in most situations. The best form of charity is prayer, and as already mentioned, prayer is free. If you're not spiritual please make it a point to be so, and prayer is an everyday occurrence not only in catastrophic situations. Also, prayer shouldn't be solely directed at others, as it is not selfish to pray for oneself. We all could use a little prayer, as we are all a work- in- progress.)

A Whole New World

These are therapists from Dodd Hall in Columbus. I had pool therapy with Adam (whose name Lisa recalled,) and the girl might be Shelly, a speech therapist. Sorry the picture is blurry, but that described my prognosis for recovery and my general state of mind, at that time!

Waking from the coma and my recovery did not happen in a quick magical snap of one's fingers. There was no magic wand used to rouse me from my comatose state. There was no "poof" sound followed by smoke. Instead, waking up was gradual and difficult. People said I was groggy, kind of like a zombie, for a couple of weeks. Doctors warned my parents that when I was waking up, I would not recognize and would not know who family members were. My parents were proud that I recognized them standing next to my hospital bed.

Doctors had informed my parents that patients with injuries similar to mine tend to use foul language when waking up. However, my accident had yet to follow the normal string of events that are expected after an accident like mine. At one point, I was lying in the hospital bed babbling nonsense. The nurses couldn't make any sense of what I was trying to say but mom and dad were tickled to listen closely and realize I was saying the Act of Contrition, a prayer that I said daily in my life. I don't recall reciting this prayer, but I think I may have been trying to make up for ten weeks of no prayer.

When I first awoke from the comatose state, I felt like I was going to be a permanent resident at the hospital. I couldn't walk or talk and I didn't even know how to begin to do these basic things. I was not allowed to eat any solids or drink any pure liquids. Doctors fed me through a tube through my side and into my stomach. I wore an enormous neck brace, and I had a tracheotomy peeking out of my neck. Normally my hands were tied to the bed so I that could not pull my tracheotomy out. On one occasion when my parents came to visit, the nurse untied my hands so they would be free for mom and dad to hold. Because the trachea tube caused discomfort, and I didn't necessarily realize the role it played in helping me breathe, I yanked it from my throat and pulled it out, cutting off my own oxygen. Luckily though, nurses quickly came into the room to reattach my oxygen supply.

I only vividly recall about three days of my stay at Dodd Hall, but it seemed like an eternity. Home was the only place I wanted to be. Even though I could not carry on a conversation with the average person, I could still communicate with Mom and Dad. I would beg and plead for Mom or Dad to please take me with them when they left for the evening. I even offered to wash and dry dishes everyday if they took me home. I now realize that I was in no condition to go home but that never stopped me from asking.

At nighttime, when nobody was monitoring me at bedside, I had to wear a bed belt. It was fastened around my waist at night so I would not fall out of bed. I liked to turn and lie on my side or stomach when I slept, but with the belt, those sleeping positions were impossible. Before my family would leave after visiting me in the hospital, they made sure that the bed belt was relatively loose so I could turn.

Frustrating, to say the least, was this recovery, and eventually I did seek to discover what all happened and how I could have prevented it from ever occurring again. At one time, I felt it was necessary to know what one has done wrong or is doing wrong in order to correct something bad. "A guy, who always strived to make improvements in any task he was doing" would be my perfect description. So it was in every fiber and sinew of me to try and figure out what happened, and how I could prevent this from ever happening again. I twisted my brain and wretched my soul trying to sort things out.

I did come to the realization that there was nothing I could have done to keep this event what is called an accident-from happening. As I was going through all the painful and annoying processes of recovery and relearning, I did recognize early on that I was very much in control of what happened next. And so, I steered forward knowing that I could not have ever practiced enough of anything to keep from getting into a serious rendezvous with a utility pole. I also recognized my time of recovery as a prime opportunity to move forward with my dreams and desire to make the absolute most of this life that I could. The difficult part for me to accept has been to truly grasp and understand that there was nothing I could have done to prevent what happened; there was no evident mistake to correct.

(Having a competitive spirit, which both of my parents instilled within me, is responsible for the fortitude I had since that fateful December day to carry on in this whole new world that I was thrown into. I may have been thrown in it, but I chose not to be thrown around. I believe that the competitiveness that my parents gave to me was the key to not only my survival, but to my complete overcoming. Complete as in where I am today. Whether you have an issue or setback, or no problem at all, there is always a way to make things better, and typically competition drives a person.   I am blessed with the kind of people who held such a strong sense of family, sibling and friendly rivalry, and competition in all areas of life.

I am highly competitive in everything that I do, but being around people and challenging them is not a constant. The stiffest competition that challenges me is this handsome face that looks at me every time I look in the mirror. I might sound a little funny or boastful at times depending on the way you see things, but be assured I'm not that way. If you're looking for challenges or a way to stay competitive, try yourself. Challenging yourself is often times the best way to move forward in difficult times. Be careful though, because if you set high standards for yourself (recommended), you must be prepared to build on your trials for next time. Success is not lost if you fail but rather when you stop trying after failure. Failure seems imminent when the standards are high. It was obvious early on through trial and error that I am in most part responsible for the rest of my life.

I used the competitive aspect as my driving force, but that is my way to stay focused. That is the best way for me to deal with everything; everything turns out to be a game, and if you must remind yourself and everybody that you are winning, then you really aren't. Winning in life is a personal standard; just go out and nonchalantly win.)

On the Road to Recovery

Finally, I was on my way to recovery! Occupational therapy (O.T.) was less painful than physical therapy, but it was not without its own difficulties. After I was helped to the wheelchair, since that was my main mode of transportation, I would take part in an O.T. session. We worked with something in my hands to make them work better. One day it was going well, I thought, until I dropped the piece we were working with. I tried to reach it from my wheelchair, but the tool was lying just beyond my reach for the way I was sitting. The chair had been customized for me so I must have been leaning one way or another making the reach difficult. Whether my therapist was trying to prepare me for the future and/or motivate me is not known, but she told me that I better learn how to pick things up from the ground now, while in my wheelchair, if I ever wanted to be able to do it. The way her sharp words came across was practically cutting down any ounce of confidence I had left. It was like she was telling me I would be in a wheelchair for the rest of my life. I brewed over that all day. I was as stubborn as an ox. I was determined to prove her wrong, just as I have wanted to prove people wrong my whole life. This time was no different. The therapist deserves some credit for motivating me to want to improve, but there is another person who played a major role in my recovery efforts.

As Dad was leaving Dodd Hall one evening, I specifically recall begging him to take me home. That was not an unusual thing for me to do, and he finally told me that if I worked hard and did as the therapists instructed, that maybe some day I would get to come home. Dad was the smartest man alive to me, and I believed everything he said. All I wanted to do was go home. For just over eight weeks I had been in Columbus, and only post-comatose for around two weeks, but it seemed like an eternity. Having stated this, I do admit that since patience is not one of my greatest virtues, it is something that I have to work on daily. Although a recovery such as this would seem like a never-ending battle for anyone, I'm sure my at-times lack of patience made the recovery process seem eternal.

Most 18-year-old boys have a craving for food, and I was not different. I could not eat normal food when I was at Dodd so it was all pureed. All of what I could eat was of a pudding-like consistency. For over ten weeks I did not have any food outside of some vitamin and nutrient concoction poured into my stomach tube, and I graciously accepted any and all food, even if it was similar to baby food in a jar.

My first word after the tracheotomy was plugged to enable talking was "water," and that seems justified. It was a while before I could have plain water. I needed to use Thick-it® which was a thickening powder, in all of my liquids because if I drank water that had not been thickened, then there was a chance it could seep into my lungs and cause pneumonia. I had a rough enough time the way it was, and pneumonia would only worsen matters. I recall nurses and mom and dad even wiping my mouth after brushing my teeth to be sure as little water as possible could make its way into my lungs. Talk about being embarrassing and frustrating. No one wants to be helpless. Yet it was what life had thrown my way, and I had to work with it and move forward, some how, some way.

(Perhaps economic issues such as a job loss had led you to a very stressful point in your life. Maybe it's a matter of not being able to stop an addiction or bad habit. Possibly you're in a relationship that seems to be sucking the life out of everyone. Whatever your situation may be, the best thing to do is to find a way to admit it and accept it. See the situation for what it truly is.

Many people go through their lives in an unhealthy relationship; for instance, trying to make another person change to be something that they want them to be. Another example could be when people keep telling themselves that their habit is not that bad or they can control it - whether it is trying to quit smoking or to eat better- because those feelings are false and self-promoting of the bad action or addiction. Yet another example could be justifying the way an employer talks to you or treats you due to the knowledge that "at least you still have a job unlike many people". These examples show that the truth has not been admitted and accepted.

Admittance and acceptance must happen before you can move forward. What are things that you have yet to admit and accept, to move forward and then to change for the better? List these out on paper or on the computer, not just in your mind. Share them with someone that you trust who can help you come up with ways to make good changes in your life. Allow them to keep you accountable by not being upset when you get their feedback and advice.)

While in Columbus I would try to get water without Thick-it from my visitors, but that never worked. It didn't make a difference whether I had juice, pop, or water, Thick-it made the drink taste bad. On the positive side, it was better than no drink at all and also beat the alternative, which could have been getting stuck with pneumonia.

I was thankful for all the visitors who came to see me. Cousins Mark and Christine came to the University Hospital every week I was there, and even when I was still in a coma, they came to show support for Mom and Dad. Remember Mark was probably my closest friend, and our growing up years had been full of companionship and competition.

In secret, my uncle and Godfather showed up early one Saturday morning and visited for a while. It wasn't really anything I was not supposed to tell somebody, but my parents were not made aware of this beforehand. Since it was a weekend, both of my parents were in Columbus, but spending the night in a hotel since Dodd Hall had no family room vacancy like St. Rita's Medical facility did. Mom said they were both worried that I had finally started to hallucinate and say things that weren't real, when I told them that Mike stopped by earlier that day. They feared that everything the medical personnel originally had told them of what could happen in cases like mine was coming true. My immediate family had arrived about 9:00 A.M. and did not believe Mike was there and left already. Medical personnel originally had been telling my parents everything that happened in cases like mine, but since they were not aware of Mike's stopping by either, they could not tell my parents. Later they learned that Mike really did stop.

Kevin Kiene also visited me a lot while I was in the Ohio State University medical facility. He was several years older than I, but he shared my love of sports. We were in the same fantasy football league in the fall of 1997, and he knew I was very interested in fantasy sports. He was big into fantasy baseball as well, and he shared his team with me that year. It truly was a kind deed that was much appreciated even though I did not know most of what was going on with the league and could not remember enough to track the information in the hospital.

Cousins Ben and Justin were also big time supporters; their brother Clint had been in my class since first grade. I was very close with all my Schroeder side relatives and saw them at least once per week. Ben and Justin were even my opponents when we had camping wars. They went to college at Ohio State and Dodd Hall was only about a ten-minute walk from their house. Even though I was unaware, Ben says they would come at random times throughout the day, often times more than once.

Two of my friends, Kelly and Andrea, wrote to Larry Bird explaining my situation. Apparently they reached another Larry Bird, not the basketball player. This nice guy with a famous name gave them the proper address to reach THE Larry Bird. They acquired an autographed 8 x 10, which proudly hangs where I see it everyday. Kelly and Andrea attended St. Anthony's grade school, like me, so we all have been friends since first grade. They were even in a group of friends that I enjoyed prom with both my junior and senior years. That picture hangs next to another signed photo of Larry Bird that I received from Dad's aunt. This second picture is also an 8 x 10, but it is an officially licensed NBA product specifically addressed, "To: Matt." My great aunt just happened to be staying at the same hotel as Mr. Bird one time, and she gave it to me after I was home for good. I cherish both pictures of Larry Bird hanging in my room, not one more than the other and not both necessarily because they have Larry Bird in them, but because they were both given by people I love.

A big group of people came after the Ohio State versus Indiana University basketball game one Saturday, in Columbus. Clinton's cousin on his mom's side of the family was Luke Recker. Clinton and I went to watch one of Luke's high school games in Indiana. I also followed his basketball successes and watched him play in the McDonald's High School All America game on television prior my accident. After he signed with Indiana and schedules came out, a big group of us planned a trip to go down to Columbus to watch the Buckeyes take on the Hoosiers. I never attended the game, but I had a slew of visitors before that game.

To keep with the basketball theme, my high school basketball coach came to visit also. Chris Grothaus gave me a big banner that was signed by the varsity team. Everyone who associated with me knew that sports, mainly basketball, played a large role in my life. I can virtually tie everybody to a sports memory.

Brian, Ryan, Clint, and Kurt, other boys named Schroeder in my class since first grade, added support to my healing process. We five had done much together, and it never failed that humor played a role in the situations we encountered. There are many more people who visited, and I wish I could list them all, but these were the most significant to me.

(Who are the people you are most thankful for in your life? Who are the ones that should get the credit for contributing to who you are today? Be sure to let them know how grateful you

are for what they have done, and specifically tell them what they have contributed. It may not be as easy for you to pull up a list of names as I have done, yet if you think about it, someone was there and is there for you. It is very important for their sake and for yours to be able to pinpoint those who have been most meaningful for you. This greatly contributes to the quality of life, thoughts, attitudes, choices, and actions that will help you to soar.)

The insurance company determined that my allotted time at the rehab center was nearing an end, and was scheduled to stop paying a week or so before I actually moved to another location. However staff in Columbus was successful in gaining another week since I was finally showing drastic improvement. In the basement of Dodd Hall there was a Wendy's restaurant, and that became a thrilling adventure for me during the last week or so I was in Columbus. My trips with parents in the evening to Wendy's are some of my few memories from the University hospital because food was a real treat for me. I was still limited to pureed foods, but special permission was granted from nurses to let me eat Wendy's iced dessert. My parents usually ordered me a large chocolate frosty. It was noted in the journal that I ate the whole thing myself. My parents were undoubtedly excited.

As the bonus week was nearing an end, my parents were preparing to send me to Waterford Commons, which was affiliated with the Medical College of Ohio (MCO) in Toledo. Dad drove me from Columbus to Toledo. My sister Lisa came along too, and the road trip was much more enjoyable to me than the daily run-through of the Dodd Hall routine. A chance to get away from the hospital and rehab center was like Christmas is to a youngster. It is true that Dad had not a round belly that shook when he laughed like a bowl full of jelly, nor even a beard of white. But Dad could be described as a jolly old elf. Happiness surrounded him because I was moving closer to home and improving on a daily basis. I have to say that I was quite happy as well. The people a person is surrounded by help create the atmosphere, and I was with Dad. I could not ask for better company.

New Surroundings

I had officially graduated from the pureed foods diet when leaving Dodd Hall. We stopped at a Burger King on the way to Waterford Commons, but it was also the first day of Lent, Ash Wednesday. Being Catholic meant that we abstained from meat on this day and other Fridays in Lent, but even no meat was better than being cooped up in some room for disabled persons. The fish and fries tasted more like steak and caviar to me. I never had caviar, but know it is supposed to be a delicacy, and the food tasted that delicious to me. The fact that it was my first real food also helped make the meal taste like a fine cuisine.

I was encouraged to take small bites and chew extremely well. I was allowed to drink true liquids again too. The traumatic brain injury had left me incapable of knowing how to swallow for a while, but I bid farewell to that Thick-it® powder concoction forever and needless to say, there were no tears shed. Can you imagine, just being thankful for pure water? Oh how we often take things in life for granted.

For the longest time I had to sit in good posture while I drank! Coughing was a regular occurrence as traces of water, juice, or pop would make their way to my windpipe. Lisa was a nurse's aid, and she was familiar with patients coughing while drinking. On the trip to Toledo, she kept checking to make sure everything was okay.

Waterford Commons was a unique place because only half of its rooms were filled with rehab patients. The other half was like a nursing home for people who were there for the rest of their lives. Dad stayed with me that first night at Waterford Commons because the new people and atmosphere were a lot to take in for a person of my condition. Luckily, Dad had visited the facility before having me stay there. Of course, I was staying in the rehab unit, but Dad did not tell me all the details surrounding the situation. It evidently was not yet known if I would ever improve enough to come home or not, and the more permanent wing of Waterford was there if my improvement came to a halt.

I was allowed to make a once-a-week 24-hour voyage homeward starting after therapy sessions on Saturdays. That first weekend I did not make it home because I had just arrived late in the week, and it was obvious that I needed to get acquainted with the building and my room. My family came to Waterford Commons to visit instead. Being in Toledo made it much easier for some people to visit. Ben and Justin were no longer a short distance away, but I had other cousins who attended Bowling Green State University, which was nearby. My cousin Jason, who attended Toledo University, was one visitor that I recalled. He is on Mom's side of the family, and we did not see each other as frequently as the Schroeder cousins did, but it was refreshing to see another familiar face.

The first meal I had at the live-in rehab center is memorable for another reason besides being back on the pureed diet. Although I got the order to be on regular food when I left Dodd Hall, evidently Waterford had not received that information. It was Ash Wednesday when I got there, as mentioned before, but the staff at this MCO branch apparently cared not about my Catholic practices. I was given some pureed meat dish to eat. I complained and demanded something different, but a non-meat meal was not offered on this day. Dad finally told me that since I was in a hospital-like atmosphere, it would be acceptable if I ate meat. Any other food discrepancies were not remembered, so I guess everything else was in my liking.

When it came time to sleep, things almost seemed unbearable. Sure, the bed in my room had all the usual controls to achieve maximum comfort level but it was only long enough for a short person. The mattress stopped, and there was a big wooden base to the bed, which came up to around my ankles. I like to be able to extend my legs out straight, but that was not very feasible with my new sleeping arrangements. Sometime during that first full week at Waterford, a longer bed was attained, but I still felt trapped at night.

Tying me in with a bed belt at night was no longer a plan of action (that was a Dodd Hall characteristic), but at Waterford Commons, there were bed rails. Maybe it is because I never used bed rails, or perhaps I was getting tired of staying away from home, but the facility's normal sized beds were also too narrow. The rails were so close together that moving around much was next to impossible. I preferred to toss and turn a bit in my sleep, but I felt like a lion in captivity. Visitors did not pay an admission fee to see me like they would have to at the zoo, but during nights, I felt that I should have a bigger cage.

When I went to Waterford Commons I still had a feeding tube in my stomach, and in order to get it removed, I had to successfully gain weight for two straight weeks. I wanted to leave nothing to chance on gaining weight. That was possibly the worst thing that could have been said because when I try to do something, I go full throttle until the goal is achieved. So we ordered a pizza or had desserts most nights for a snack. When the two weeks were up and I was successful in steadily putting on the pounds, I could not stop eating. I put on quite a few pounds - too many in Toledo.

There was a balloon attached to the end of the tubing that was inside my stomach. That way the tube could not be bumped out unintentionally. After about one full week of careful monitoring both food and fluid intake and output, medical staff determined that it would be safe to remove the peg from my stomach.

When a person gets a shot while visiting their doctor, the nurse usually informs them that they will experience a mild pain or feel a prick. The discomfort is usually mild and barely gets noticed. Before that stomach peg was removed, I was informed that there might be a little pain, and I figured it would be like getting a shot. To take that tube out, a suction piece was used. My skin had attached to the tube at the point of insertion, and there was probably some pain coming from inside my body too. When coupled with the feeling of skin tearing away at the point of insertion, it was the most excruciating physical pain that I could imagine

The whole process only lasted a couple of minutes, but that can be described as the worst two minutes of my entire recovery. I would have rather endured a thousand shots, but it was nowhere near as hard to take as the mental pain I would endure.

The mental anguish was taking shape in Toledo at Waterford Commons. I had a terrible time allowing people to see me like this, helpless and in a state of need. I had been proud to do things for myself or for other people (for example, for my groups of friends or my old basketball team). Yet now I was forced to grit my teeth and welcome help. Friends and family are often willing to assist you in times of crisis, but I had never been through a situation quite like this before, so it was hard to start asking for things. Coming home on the weekends from my new base in Toledo was much anticipated and welcomed as can be surmised, but deep down it put me in my place, too. Before all of this, things seemed to come easier for me than the average person as I made choices and took actions to make them happen. Although it was a habit and desire for me to encourage people to do the same, "mind over matter", the daily minute details that I had to endure can't possibly be put in words. I started to realize that the world as I knew it before was no longer.

On weekends when I went home, it was great to finally see people from my community. Although the locals understood that being unable to do things smoothly or solely was not yet possible for what I had endured, it still had me feeling somewhat like a parasitic leech. No one likes to be required to go through and relearn what you mastered as a child, and no one likes to have to depend on others for things such as learning how to talk, going to the bathroom and so on. It was a very humbling experience, to say the least.

(This brings to mind life phases and experiences that we all have to go through, whether we like it or not. Most people won't have to go through a devastating car accident recovery, yet we all have to go through such things as aging. People usually look upon aging as a negative thing; something that they resent. I can understand why. Losing your hair, perhaps having increased health issues, not being able to do what you used to, watching your physical appearance "decline", and more aren't usually things that people anticipate with joy. In fact, many groan and complain about what stinks about getting older. Yet, similar to the steps I had to endure and to take, aging can be something that you choose to help drive you even more. The process of aging (and other phases in life such as a bad relationship, money problems, job losses, a child who is rebellious, etc.) can push you to be a self-starter and allow you to not only embrace tasks, but to celebrate them, and grow on every level. Or they can be times and factors in your life that can bring you down on every level, bit by bit or in a fast, furious way. Once again, it's a matter of choice. Accept, embrace, and celebrate or don't accept, don't find reasons to celebrate, and miss out on the amazing celebration of having chances to grow? I encourage you to party like a rock star, in this case! Please visit my website's blog for inspirational messages on how to accept and overcome the challenges of life – www.mattschroeder.org.)

Instead of allowing a victory by the battle of my mind, the mental anguish that was taking place at Toledo Waterford Commons, I chose to push myself that much harder to be as I was before. My therapy at Waterford was not simple or easy. Granted, having therapy now, it would be a walk in the park since I currently move with ease, but to do those tasks at the time was like trying to make a basket while navigating from coaster to coaster at Cedar Point. Those carnival-type rims are much smaller than normal and require almost a perfect shot in order to win.

However that flawless performance is what I always sought, and tough therapy sessions were not different here from anywhere else.

I even was warned not to get so worked up and excited when doing sessions, but I felt that I wanted to show everybody that I could return near to where I was before the accident. Injuries never kept me down before, and there was no reason to figure now was different. Yet it was extremely frustrating, to say the least, to try and get others to see that I was the same. I did not know then yet, but now I welcome and feel appreciative of what my long road to recovery has taught me. Even the fateful December day of my senior year is a blessing, for it made me who I am today. It's given me more patience, rather forced it on me, and patience was my extremely weak point. And that's just one thing that that the tragedy has caused me to work on. I am even thankful for the worst of the worst that was yet to come: kidney failure, dialysis, removal gone bad, transplant, having to relearn how to do things all over again. All these things I am thankful for.

I never used to think about my health or how others dealt with health issues. I was so used to feeling great every day and being able to do all the athletic and physical things that I did. Yet the recovery process has left me a changed person. It's amazing how we tend to take the smallest things for granted until life changes on a dime for us.

(Yeah! My first word was "water". Before all this happened, I really never thought of water other than when I was thirsty. Yet water was what consumed my thoughts for the longest time during the recovery processes. But I also knew that the natural form of water could have killed me at one time if it went into my lungs. All those years before the accident, I took

water for granted. Now looking back after the car accident and recovery, I can see lots of other things that I took for granted.

What do you take for granted? Do you take for granted the ability to sit or stand, eat or drink, and walk and talk, run and shout without even thinking about these things? I think most do, and I did too. But after not being able to do these things for a long time after a transformer transformed my life in an accident, I have a much greater respect for these activities and abilities. Ponder upon just the mere basic functioning and how just one twist in life can forever change it all, and your appreciation in life will be much greater. Now think of more important things like relationships. Flying a kite with your friends is great, and by flying a kite I mean doing anything with others. Just the thought of a sudden illness or car wreck which can change it all – from the basic act of walking to a personal relationship – will help you put things into focus. Please e-mail message me with things that you will try to no longer take for granted in your life. Also please give thanks to whatever or whoever you think deserves it.)

Therapy, Therapy, and Did I Mention Therapy?

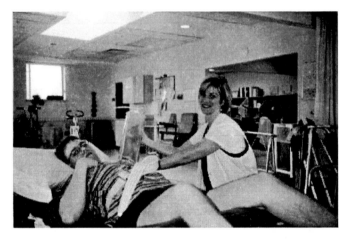

Therapeutic gym at Waterford Commons. Notice in the background, there are many items used for tiring physical therapies. This one was a relaxing occupational therapy session working with my arm.

My first weekend homecoming was a huge moment of celebration. As Mom and I pulled in, I was surprised but excited because our driveway was packed with cars. A bunch of my classmates were there to welcome me back. It was a good feeling to see so many of my school friends offering their support away from the classroom. They all stuck around until late afternoon or early evening, and I did more listening than talking. Speech was something that I still had to work on, and it made me very tired. Tired was a good thing because I wore myself out visiting with my classmates, which is a grand thing. All the people and commotion can be attributed to my cousins Clint and Kurt who kept everyone at school updated on my situation.

When everyone dispersed, I needed sleep, and I did not do much else that evening. The excitement of my trip home was not over yet because I attended 8:30a.m. Mass on Sunday morning at Saint Anthony's. I got to use the elevator at church, which was installed a year or two before my accident. Father Keith made a big deal about seeing me at church in his announcements at the closing of mass. Everyone in church applauded, but that was just the beginning of my excitement that morning. We went to my grandparents' house after 8:30 mass for donuts and juice.

Typically, several of my Grandparent's children (my aunts and uncles) would come over to Grandma's house (Grandpa was there too but it was easier and routine to not include his name) on Sunday mornings after early Mass and Sunday evenings after dinner. My first weekend home was no different. Most of my aunts, uncles, and cousins were present Sunday morning, and even though most of the family already had seen me at one place or another, they were still happy to see me again. I would be back to Waterford Commons by late afternoon. Even though the experience of the first weekend in Grove was short lived, it made me feel more like a human being and less like a patient.

Back at Waterford Commons, I got settled into my bed with side rails and was ready for another week. The second full week was similar to the first, but it seemed much easier knowing that homeward I would go the next weekend for one day. I had cousins and friends come to visit me at Toledo as they did in

Columbus. Amy and Beth were my cousins, who went to Bowling Green State University, and they visited often like Ben and Justin did in Columbus. Bowling Green was not as close to Waterford as Dodd was to Ohio State, but nonetheless, the short drive made visitations very attainable.

Amy was studying to be a physical therapist and at the time, I detested physical therapy and anybody associated with it. I knew they were actually helping and trying to get me better quickly, but sometimes we did some painful things. Beth was studying speech pathology, and she sat in on some of my therapy sessions. They both came often to visit with me.

I had speech, occupational, and physical therapy sessions like before, but time seemed to pass relatively quickly. The daily routine dragged on, yet going home each weekend made it sit better with me. Speech therapy was like my break, which was much needed after a session of physical or occupational therapy. The break was quite necessary after wearing me out from the other therapies, but speech itself was very frustrating at times. One would think in speech therapy a person would do a bunch of talking. I loved to talk, but it sounded more like mumbling because I could not enunciate well enough yet. Instead we did different sorts of mouth exercises.

Physical therapy was not a whole lot different from Dodd Hall except for the fact that there was no pool at this MCO branch. I know that I did a lot of cardiovascular work in the room designated for exercise. I remember riding a stationary bike for the first time since the car wreck, but it was not the way I remembered exercising on a bicycle. It was a bike that could be operated with your arms, either simultaneously with the legs or alone. I was instructed to use only my hands, and I was always told to slow down, because my heart rate would get too high. I am a go-getter and had to be monitored so I would not go too fast. I guess the technique was more important than speed.

We also practiced walking at Waterford, and at first, it was just standing while holding on to something. Then we alternated standing on one foot, and finally we moved to using a walker. One time I remember walking all the way to my room after therapy, which was only about 50 meters from the exercise room. That was probably during the last few days I was in Toledo, and that distance for someone just learning to walk again, did seem like a marathon. That had my parents and me extremely excited because I was slowly but surely making progress. At this time we already knew that I was coming home at the end of the week.

After 3 ½ weeks in Toledo, a meeting with therapists, parents, and me to discuss my progress was held, and we were going to discuss going home. It was a big day for me because all I ever wanted to know was when I could stay at home on a full time basis. It was determined that in two weeks I could live with my parents full time, if I would continue improving at the same rate. We were all excited about my coming home for more than a 24-hour period. I was so focused on two weeks that the wait seemed longer, but I still had two more weekends. I do not remember which weekend but one of them was prom.

(And there I was longing to go HOME. Yet many of you reading this may not want to come home, have been away from home for a while, or may not want to have anything to do with home. Whatever your case may be and for whatever reasons you may have, I suggest that you make an effort to long for home. Home may mean your friends. It may mean something that you fantasized such as a healthy home life or it may even mean a

wonderful past, yet for certain reasons you're not as connected to home as you used to be. Make it a point to draw up memories, thoughts, and actions to bring back home and to make the people and place that you consider home to be exactly that. You can indeed create the life that you want to have, and it all does start with the mind. There is a popular quote that says, "Mind over matter" and life really is about this.)

It was a good thing that I could leave Waterford for one day each weekend, because it was necessary for me that I go to my senior prom. I was happy to be able to have a part of what most high schoolers get to do – Prom Time! Prom was an event I thought I'd never be able to attend, yet amazingly, I <u>was</u> able to attend. As a senior, I attended prom with most of the same people that I had attended junior prom. We all wore tuxedos (the guys did at least), as is the custom for prom, and surely we looked like a dapper crew. My senior year, students were required to eat our meal at the prom, and maybe that was a blessing in disguise. I was not using my left arm much yet, and the one armed bandit, me, often times made a mess. I might have caused a scene in a restaurant if we were there. I never made a mess, but felt reassured that if I had, my classmates would understand.

I begged and pleaded to take my walker along to use only part time, but was turned down by my parents; I ended up taking my wheelchair. I asked people if they cared to let me stand up to slow dance with them, but everyone was too concerned with my safety. I did get to dance with many from my wheelchair though. It seemed as though everyone was elated to see me. The prom server girls pushed me in my wheelchair into the gymnasium. Nobody wanted to, nor would, hold my arms and let me stand for a picture like I thought, but my thoughts and opinions were not agreeable with the way things were done. Many people shared stories and took pictures with me. It made me feel like I was just the regular me, but what I soon discovered made me feel weird.

At the senior prom put on by the grade below us, we each had a program sitting by our plate, but I did not look at it until after the meal. Food was one of my greatest treats ever since I was allowed to eat real food, and elegant edibles were brought in by some classy catering service. After the meal I looked at the program and then the atmosphere became confusing. The back of the paper said something about the junior class dedicating the 1998 Prom to Matt Schroeder, and there I was reading it. It gave me a strange feeling.

I could not figure why the prom was dedicated to me. Things are usually dedicated to people who are dead, not people who are alive. My first thought was that, apparently, everybody doubted what God could do for me. I was a bit angered but not for long. I understood that people were judging my outcome by the wrecked car they saw sitting uptown and by what my cousins saw at the hospital. The outcome could not have been very bright when prom was planned. I guess it makes me feel good that people were thinking of and, likely, praying for me. But I think the programs should have been changed when they heard I was, for sure, going to be there. I guess nothing was for sure, especially when I was trying to endure rehabilitation.

(Readers, I suggest never to assume as I did for a bit during this strange prom incident. As you can see, I quickly sorted things out in my mind based on the determination that from others' standpoint, chances looked grim that I would survive, let alone actually make it, to prom. My moments of confusion, which turned into anger, disappeared as I made the

choice to see from their perspective. Never assume. Making assumptions only leads to consequences that may not be good due to acting and reacting on what is not proven to be the truth. As the saying goes, "The truth will set you free."

No matter how intense or life-changing your situation may be, try to keep some sort of normalcy and balance. I wanted so badly to attend my prom and with the circumstances, this would normally not be something that was achievable. However, because everyone chipped in to make this happen, I was able to enjoy the wonderful things in life without allowing the negatives of my circumstances to disrupt one of those joys.)

Life is Therapy

Jamie, Kim, Jenny, and Jennifer surround me at senior prom.
We had all been classmates since first grade.

So prom was over and it was back to therapy, therapy, and even more therapy. One more facet of my day that I have yet to touch upon was occupational therapy. How ironic it is that occupational therapy is what I have the most memories from. True that in Columbus, it was what my therapist told me: how she thought about my future that made me want to prove the critics wrong. Yet conversations with therapists were a little different in Toledo. As I was starting to feel better and coming home on weekends, humor started to return in my life. My family, as mentioned before, is very comical, and I was quite the jokester before the wreck that nearly took my life.

The following incident reassured everyone that I had not lost my sense of humor and was well on the way to returning to the Matt that they once knew. One day in occupational therapy, the therapist told me that if I continued to keep working as hard as I had been, that I would be able to do most things that require two hands fine. I keenly asked her if I would be able to play the piano. She said "yes", and I affirmed her of the coolness of that fact because I never knew how to play the piano before the accident. There were yet more times that humor entered my thinking. It was good to be laughing at things in life again.

Cousin Beth used to joke around with me when she came to visit, which was about every weekday. I would occasionally ask her to get me something like an extra pillow or glass of water because I was still bedridden and needed the nurse's help to transfer to the wheelchair. When I first asked for her assistance, she responded with something about hearing the magic words, and I knew those were "please" and "thank you". Yet Beth's magic words were "right now." She was just trying to get a reaction from my parents. I informed them of Beth's magic words; however, the two-word phrase did not work on them, needless to say.

I loved to use the phone at Waterford Commons, and two more mildly humorous instances involving Alexander Graham Bell's invention occurred on April 1, 1998. It snowed light flurries on that day, and Dad was up to visit me and is responsible for my first April fool's prank. I called home that evening and told Mom that he would be spending the night up here because it was snowing something terrible. She probably knew that something was fishy but played along anyhow, and after I told her, "April Fool's", Dad spoke to her briefly. He was trying to get Mom back for the prank we pulled on him more than a decade ago when we met him for lunch and had him believing that the basement was flooded.

The second April Fool's call was also made that evening. It was my idea to call the Pizzeria in Columbus Grove. I ordered a large pizza with sausage and pepperoni on the pan style crust for delivery to Waterford Commons in Toledo. When the girl who answered the phone said she was sorry, but they did not deliver that far, I was stunned that this person did not know who I was. I asked to speak to the manager, and Curt Shafer was put on the phone. He recognized my voice right away and said that the girl who answered the phone was a new worker still in training. I guess that is why she didn't know who I was. Surprisingly, I had thought that I knew and worked with all of the employees.

There was, however, another reason for the call. When I started eating regular food, my uncle Karl once brought a pizza to my room in Toledo. The drive was more than one hour so Curt Shafer let them use a delivery bag to keep it warm. Karl said Curt did not charge him for the pizza because he was informed that Karl was bringing it to me. I had to personally thank Curt for sending the best pizza money could buy although this pizza was given to my uncle.

(Indeed, laughter is the best medicine. Perhaps you're not the type to find it in many situations in life, yet it's important to

find some humor. If you can't seem to find it, be sure to create it. Studies have shown that humor and laughter keeps us healthy, hopeful, and all those other positive things. Plus it helps us to take others and ourselves less seriously, which produces great results. I encourage you to find the joy of life each day. Please email me with some of your comical moments and memories. I'd love to share a chuckle or two. matt@mattschroeder.org.)

We also tried other practical activities in occupational therapy. We even practiced dressing and tying shoes alone. I was eventually able to get shorts on myself using the bed to lie on, but tying shoes was next to impossible. It was not fun to have other people tie my shoes in public, but there was no shame with others helping with what I could not do by myself. I also practiced bathing by myself.

A nice warm shower was relaxing before bed. Rubbing shampoo in my hair with my left hand was a way to have therapy during a shower. It was truly difficult to use my left arm, but I used any chance to gain better usage of it. Many times my parents pointed out the success of people with usage of just one arm using wheelchairs, but most of these people had their disabilities since birth. My parents tried to keep my morale up because it was still not known if I would ever walk again unassisted. It was a nice gesture by them, but I was determined to gain full recovery.

(Are there some things that you want to do in life? Perhaps there are things that you need to do. It is only by determining that you will achieve what you want and need to do that will give you what it takes to accomplish these goals. Determination, like many things in life, is a choice.)

Keep on keeping on!

Without a doubt, playing a game of basketball or shooting hoops had been part of my daily routine, and the therapists were informed of this. It is always important that the things people love to do and that are a part of their daily routine are added to their therapy agendas. That way each patient can get back as close to their full and normal life as possible so that they can "keep on keeping on".

Fortunately, at Waterford Commons there was a basketball court outside and my parents and therapists worked hard to make my life as normal as it used to be before the accident. We went out to shoot baskets once in occupational therapy, but I could not get the motion the therapist was looking for, so once was enough for the therapists. It upset me as well, not being able to shoot the basketball. Frustrated is how I felt, and my inability to shoot hoops was due to my arms not having enough strength and my head not being able to balance sufficiently even with a walker and support from two therapists. That frustration may have contributed to the cause of why we only went out only once. The last thing anybody wanted was for me to feel dejected.

Back in Columbus I wore a gait belt whenever I had to be transferred, and there was no difference in Toledo. It was used whenever I was practicing with the walker too. Mom and Dad were instructed on how to properly use the gait belt. It had to be used on the weekends that I came home for a temporary visit. I tried to use the walker as much as possible, but I was not able to walk when we went places, and I tired quickly. Another very frustrating thing was that I often wet the bed at night, but my bladder control at night was improving.

When I came home from Waterford Commons the first time, there were a lot of classmates to welcome me back, but that was only for 24 hours. Cousin's Kurt, Clint, and Mark were there when I came home for good, and Mark brought his classmate Jill with him. I think cousin Christine was there too, because more often than not she was with Mark. Jill was a friend of Marks that I knew, and it was nice of her to greet me home, too. We five cousins often hung out together before I nearly lost my life, and I am grateful especially for these four people. I shared many events with them in the past, and some of them will not be shared. Do not confuse what I am saying; I am thankful for ALL of my cousins and appreciate ALL of the visitors.

At the time my accident happened, remember that I was about midway through my senior year at Columbus Grove high school, and I had been a student athlete who earned excellent grades. I was determined to receive the highest grade point average possible at my school. To graduate with honors was something that was always in my plans. I had enough completed courses and received credits to graduate with a regular diploma, but I did not work hard the first three and a half years of high school to receive a G.E.D. I worked for honors and was determined to graduate with them and receive an authentic diploma.

Since I came home from Waterford for good on Good Friday, there was not a lot of time to finish my coursework. Advanced English 12 and Art 1 were needed to fulfill requirements and graduate with an honors diploma. Believe me when I tell you that I was no Picasso and, surely, the sculpture completed by me was anything but pretty. However, it fulfilled what the art teacher saw as necessary to get credit for the course. Papers and projects were completed for school when I first came home, but at the same time, it was critical to get cracking on therapy.

Therapy started on Monday. So the first time therapy did not run its normal course was Saturday morning. I normally had Sundays off and Easter was spent like my previous 18 years were, at my Grandparents' house. Therapy started immediately the next day because a setback would be detrimental. Everybody told me how quickly I was improving, but, honestly, time moved so slowly for me that I failed to see daily improvement.

I had speech, occupational, and physical therapies, and I could neither walk nor talk yet. My left arm was always bent at the elbow with a clinched fist hanging around my waist. I was basically a cripple who only had use of his one arm. When strangers saw me in public when I did begin speaking, undoubtedly, they thought I was retarded or something. My speech was very slow and drawn out. I hated the way people would whisper amongst themselves when looking at me and hearing me speak. Sometimes bystanders would speak loudly and slowly to me as if I could not understand them if they spoke normally. I wasn't too keen on this and wanted to improve significantly before starting college in the fall, not for these strangers who looked at me like I was stupid, but for myself. I said "stupid" with the utmost respect because years later during the summer in 2005 I was a counselor at a camp for mentally challenged people. Each week at Camp Echoing Hills, Sunday late morning through Friday afternoon, we counselors were assigned typically between three and five new campers that we considered as our responsibility for six days.

Let me be clear by letting you know that these campers were not physically and/or mentally normal. Nine different weeks with nine different groups of people, plus an initial week of training and certifications, made those ten weeks rank high on a hypothetical list of most difficult periods to endure. Surprisingly enough, it was also one of the most rewarding segments of my life. Regularly we counselors were the caretakers of our specific campers, and that regularly had us doing personal care and hygiene tending that were not fun. We were never supposed to utter the word "retarded," even while horsing around with co-counselors during our day off, because all too often that term gets used in a degrading way.

Although many of these physically or mentally challenged campers were literally retarded, friendships were developed leaving us sad to see some of them go. Just because somebody's life is drastically different than yours or mine does not mean they should be loved less or treated poorly. My own temporary inability to communicate after my accident helped me understand the feelings of some campers. I related well with others who had mobility or movement issues, too. While working at camp I had many unique experiences and some funny ones, too. Everyday of my life has moments that are seen as humorous to me, but there are two similar specific events, both of which happened at a time when people were arriving at camp. When meeting the campers assigned to me, I was supposed to greet them and welcome them to Cabin 8 where I was a counselor with four or so co-counselor guys. A couple of my campers who mistook what I was doing there, asked me who my counselor was. That brought back memories of times when watching games, dancing, or just having fun with friends in bars or clubs.

I don't drink alcohol, and when people hear me speak, depending on the hour or setting, they sometimes think I am mentally challenged, although not so much now that my speech has improved with time. When people think you are playing with a few cards short of a full deck, you get treated differently. I do not place blame on those bar and club working people who confronted me formerly for thinking that I had way too much to drink, nor do I blame the campers for initially thinking I was a camper in cabin 8, because I sounded a lot like them.

In hindsight, this is funny but frustrating, too. The people we were taking care of didn't pick up on details that clued the regular person in and let them know that my nametag said "Counselor Matt". Maybe they couldn't read that or see that my t-shirt was like the rest of the cabin leaders. The campers, because of their deficiencies, were not in the know. If a person is classified as retarded, please treat them with the respect that you would treat any friend.

Surely, I was not a pleasure for my therapists to work with, at least not when I started outpatient rehab. Meetings were held every so often with my therapists, my parents, and me. I did not like to have Dad or Mom hear how stubborn I had been in therapy. I guess I was being stubborn about being stubborn. Ha! Ha!

The sessions where I was most troublesome were during speech therapy. I badly wanted to sound normal but was frustrated with the lack of talking practice. Speech was like basketball, which I later understood, and one has to learn the fundamentals before they are ready to play. Similarly, I had to strengthen muscles in my mouth and practice different movements with the tongue before I was ready to talk better. It was frustrating, and I was stubborn at times, as I had to relearn things that I had learned all over again. It wasn't fun to relearn how to do things that we normally learn as toddlers and young children. Yet all the while I was very thankful to have the opportunity of each new day and each step toward healing.

(As humans we are imperfect, and it is hard to admit our flaws. Even if everyone around us is telling us about these imperfections, we often don't want to hear it and will refuse to own up to them. No one likes to be told that they are stubborn or about any actions and character traits that aren't positive. Yet these are opportunities of growth if we allow them to be. It was not fun to listen to others tell me that I was stubborn, and it was definitely no walk in the park to have to hear this being told to my parents, the ones who I looked up to and the ones who I wanted to make proud. Yet as gruesome as it was, I had to endure it and admit that I wasn't the best person to work with at times. I tried to do better to cooperate as everyone was only trying to help. So I'd like to encourage you to admit to areas in which you are stubborn or not so grateful and work on seeing it from the viewpoint of others who are attempting to give you help. They will not be perfect, as none of us humans are, but usually, there is a something you can learn from situations that you don't like to hear about.)

To be able to walk was also my great desire, but physical therapy was like speech in that we never seemed to do what I most wanted to do. We needed to get the rest of my body up to par first. I had to build some muscle and get my posture and mechanics down. Every once in awhile a wheelchair-bound person who could speak well could be found; at that time I was not bipedal, rather four wheeled, and was not speaking very well yet either. To see those who were in a wheelchair who could speak well drove me insane. Speaking was what I saw as the most important at the beginning, and walking took a secondhand role.

Occupational therapy was the easiest of the three sessions, but I never wanted to do the small detailed oriented things that were on the agenda. However, refusing to cooperate was not done much either. Laura was my occupational therapist and I eventually termed her my drill sergeant. She ran a no-nonsense session, and the things she wanted me to do were accomplished. She was definitely my most remembered therapist and as you will later see, the only therapist that I had interactions with periodically after outpatient rehab ended.

(It's amazing the lifelong friendships that can develop from those one-time termed strangers. In my case, this therapist was like a stranger who came as an angel to help me recover. Yet who knew that we would become friends and remain friends? There is a saying to treat strangers kindly as you never know when you are entertaining angels. I never really thought about my therapists other than how they were helping me to recoup and recover, yet it is nice to know that someone from many years ago, who I thought was such a drill sergeant, would turn out to be the one I remember the most – in a nice way.

People you may not know now very well or may not even know at all may touch your life in a long-lasting way. Work at each new acquaintance, friendship, and relationship. It might mean a little to you but it could mean a lot to you and to that person some day.)

Home at Last

My family also had to work very hard taking care of me at home. There were at least three months at home where I was not able to control my bladder well at night. However, things were not quite as simple as with a child. I could not walk, so a urinal was used. Mom came whenever I called, and sometimes I would spill the urinal before she came to empty it. One time I forgot to seek help, and a wet mess was made when the urinal overflowed in bed. Frequently I woke up prior to going so the mess usually happened with the use of the urinal. The problem passed by college time, but my mom deserves a big thank you here as I know my bed sheets were washed sometimes thrice per week.

(They say that you never quite appreciate your mother until you have your own children. I say that all of us should be extremely thankful to our moms, as we may never know all the things that they do behind the scenes to make life easier and better for us. Even if your mother was not a "good mom", and perhaps she didn't even raise you in the right way or didn't even raise you at all, she still is your mother. I know this is easier said than done, yet respect her and try to find ways to love her and

thank her because she gave you life. She is your mother, after all. And moms deserve that respect just because they are Mom. I encourage you to call you mom just to say "hello." Maybe you haven't talked to her in a while, or even years, and you may not want to even now. Or you're afraid that she won't want to hear from you. Whatever the case may be, make the effort to contact your mom. It will not only be a healing step toward your relationship, but for you, a part of "The rest is up to you".)

I always tried to look at the positive aspects about my life since I came home because my parents tried to keep me thinking optimistically. They hoped and prayed that I would eventually relearn to walk but continued to show me examples of successful people who did not walk, because nobody knew if or when I would be able to walk again. Being unable to walk without assistance had some advantages. One instance clearly sticks out in my memory. Sometime in the fall of 1999, all the males from Dad's side of the family who were high school age and older went to a Chicago Bears two-day weekend getaway. I was still in a wheelchair, but that did not stop me from having fun. The tailgating section was far away from the stadium, but it didn't bother me since I was pushed to the game. The handicapped seating section was field level beside where the teams go to their locker rooms. Cousin Justin was the only person who was allowed to sit with me. However, we still had a blast. We had field level seats near the action of the game and those were better than where my family was seated. The Bears lost the game which was the best scenario for me because I was the only person rooting for the other team. I am one who likes to cheer for the opposite team of everyone else I am with. In professional sports, I am a Cincinnati fan. And let me tell you, the 1990's decade was a painful time period to be Bengal faithful.

The day of high school graduation was exciting. I was in a wheelchair and although I wanted to take the walker, my wish was overruled. My cousins pushed my chair in the processional because they, too, were graduating so nobody looked out of place, well except there was just one graduate not walking. To this day I remember that I received a two-minute standing ovation when I received my diploma. That was really a great feeling to see and hear the applause. At least to my knowledge, that was the only standing ovation by all the spectators for an individual in Columbus Grove high school history.

Although I was tackling outpatient rehabilitation after leaving Waterford Commons and I finished, then graduated high school with my classmates, I still had ambitions to be all that I could be. (Even though "Be all that you can be" was the army motto in advertisements, be assured that entering the U.S. Army was not one of my interests before the wreck or afterward.) I had planned to attend the Ohio State University in Lima for one year and then go to the main campus, in Columbus for my remaining studies in engineering.

College

Several graduates from the class of 1998: standing: Chad, Kurt, Clint, Brian. Seated: Linda, Kelly, me, Emily, Andrea. We were all friends since first grade.

That initial summer after my accident, most of my time was spent in a wheelchair, which gave me a lot of thinking time. My biggest hurdles were speaking clearly and walking without assistance, and although I had head trauma, spending time in thought, analyzing situations, and deriving plans of action were not hard to do. I spoke and moved slower than your average

100

person and that problem still presents itself at times, but that only allowed time to think things through carefully. We had plans, my cousins, my friends, and I, and we had been already hypothetically writing on the chalkboard, but the chalk broke in half when it was my turn to write. I figured that my plan could still be achieved, with hard work and determination, and I was ready for anything.

I knew college would be extremely difficult given my scenario, but instead of seeing it as something so amazingly overwhelming, I chose to see reality as an exciting challenge. Going to the big city after one year locally was a tall order that would require continued hard work and drastic recovery. I was up for that challenge.

One day, Lisa did not have any urgent work to complete, so my sister took me to Saint Anthony's school to visit my former teachers because I thought my junior high instructors, as opposed to high school or college instructors, had made the most significant impact on my life. The visit had me reminiscing about my education; I felt that the junior high grades were also where I was challenged the most and learned that hard work can make both life and education go smoother.

I decided right then that I wanted to mold lives for the better like Mrs. Reichenbach and Mrs. Schroeder (seventh and eighth grade teachers, respectively) did with mine. One could get an elementary education Bachelor's and Master's degree near home at the Ohio State University in Lima. Even though I was up for the limited mobility challenge of going to Columbus after one year near home to pursue engineering, I decided to achieve an education degree and live at home. I would be going to the same school as my cousins but just at different locations after the first year, and that would be following part of the plan. Furthering my education at the Lima branch of Ohio State was not without difficulties or struggles, however.

Although it may seem like I'm rambling on and on about the past, I believe that the past helps to mold us and helps to define who we are today. In stating this, as I was deciding upon the direction of my future, I returned to the experiences of my past. It's not that I can't let go of the past. It's more that I was finding inspiration, learning, and using what I had learned from my past. At that moment of sorting out my educational future, I leaned to the two teachers who inspired me the most, and I knew that this was the course I wanted to take for my life.

(Having stated this, many people (especially in this economic crisis) are searching for a job or a better job. With many cut backs and layoffs, thousands of people are in the similar situations asking themselves, "What do I want to do when I grow up? What career should I get into? What major should I go into now that I have to decide for college?" Some are looking for another path, whether professional or personal, trying to figure out what they want to do with their lives; what they want to be. There are many books, websites, and programs on the market that try to help you "learn how to become this or that" or "find your next profession" and so on. So people wrack their brains searching for their new lives, whether it's their dream jobs, dream significant other, dream retirement, etc. There's not really a huge need to do so much searching. It's already there. What I'm saying is that you already have it in you to easily find the answers you're searching for. Just look to your past and your present.

If you're trying to find out what new job you'd be best at, instead of going to some extreme, say, from being a construction worker to enrolling in law school to be an attorney, or from being a housewife/domestic engineer to being a CEO of a large international corporation, look at your overall past plus present. If you've always done some form of manual labor and handiwork, then perhaps leaning toward being a consultant in the construction industry is something that you'll love doing. This will allow you to continue in the field that you are an expert in with much experience yet be able to move out of the physical labor part of it and into the mind/intellectual part of this industry.

Basically, what I'm suggesting is to look to what you loved to do, who inspired you, what motivated you, what you're constantly doing in your spare time, and what you think about in the back of your mind all the time. These are the things that are your passion. Looking at the past and growing and learning from it will help you make better decisions easily and quickly.)

Challenges commenced as my right hand started to tremor mildly later that summer. My right hand was definitely dominant, but it began to twitch uncontrollably when fine motor skills such as writing were attempted. This affected more than just schoolwork, but it negatively affected most things. Simple things that everyone took for granted suddenly were hard. Eating with my dominant hand was next to impossible, and I used utensils with my left hand. That was not appreciated but accepted. The most irritating effect of my shaky hand was with liquids. I accepted drinking water with my left hand, but it infuriated me to not be able to hold a glass of liquid steady enough with either hand while I walked back to my seat without spilling it.

The constant tremors were only problem-causing when I was writing or doing something that needed intricate detail. Given my situation and status in the aftermath of the accident, I could deal with a shaky hand, but I still wish something could be done. I tried to regain some normalcy in my skills by writing with my left hand, and the writing was legible, but was also a very time-consuming process.

I went to the neurologist, whom I credited with saving my life, seeking a solution to the shakiness, but nothing was ever done to combat the problem. The neurologist said there was no surgery that guaranteed success at curing my tremors. He said some experimental procedure could be tried, but that would involve major surgery and possibly permanent setbacks. I did consider it, that's why I had made the appointment, but it was easy to make a decision.

I beat the odds after the first surgery and trying another risky operation, which could result in some paralysis, was not something I was willing to gamble with. I do love taking chances, but not on something as precious as life. Dad felt the same way as I did, which was the ultimate reassurance to me, and to throw the idea of risky surgery out the window was fine with me.

School was going to be difficult while juggling therapy sessions at the same time, and getting to the right places at the correct times was going to be difficult since I was not able to drive. My sister, parents, and cousins were responsible for getting me to where I had to be at the right times. The simultaneous therapy schedule was adjusted to my class schedule. I had received a 29 on my ACT and was granted a university scholarship from the Ohio State University, but that was all before the accident. I did receive a Buckeye scholar award, which helped curb tuition costs.

One class was all I was going to take the first quarter, and there was no question that it was going to be a math course because that had always been my favorite subject. I was already enrolled in a calculus course through OSU in high school, but it was cut short due to my car mishap. Dad took me to get placement tested for math. I didn't remember all the calculus formulas and methods as shown on my examination, but the college faculty was surprised that I actually placed in a second level math course. There were two noncredit courses and one course for credit that I tested out of, but Dad and I decided to sign up for the class that I supposedly tested above. He did not want to get me flustered, and he thought that this would be a good chance to get acquainted with the college atmosphere.

The people at outpatient rehab did not think that I would do very well in college, and their assumptions were based on other brain injury patients. As I said before, there are few things where I am like everyone else. I am my own person. I even had people questioning why I was even going to school after I had my wreck. A college education was what I was seeking, and nothing was going to stop me.

(You are your own person too. With all your uniqueness, there should be no reason why you should settle for ordinary when you can be extraordinary! Never forget that and do not go by what people assume. Do what you are meant to uniquely do and be.)

The first day I was in my wheelchair and Dad took me to school. The first thing we did was check where my class was, and after he helped me to the third floor, he was gone until it was over. That was the first time that I was in a classroom during a lesson since Friday December 5, the first half of my senior year, nine months earlier. It was also the first time I met my note taker. School took some getting used to.

Ohio State's disability services office provided an individual who was already taking the class with carbon copy notebooks so that I would have a copy of his notes. Students would also get paid a little in gift certificates that were valid only at the campus bookstore. It was not a large payment, but the student did not have to put forth that much effort either. If you would call sitting near the front by me some sort of punishment, then maybe it took a little suffering on their end because that is all they would have to do for me.

Disability services also provided other important things like wheelchairs on campus if somebody needed them, but I had my own custom built chair that I used the first day. They also had the ability to get books on tape for a person. I only had one audio book from there ever, but there were more if I needed them. Mr. Craig Steven Higgins was in charge of all of Ohio State's disability services, and I became good friends with Steve, which is what Mr. Higgins preferred to be called. In second place of importance to providing note takers, scribes who would write down the answers that I dictated for testing were also provided. It worked best if somebody familiar with mathematics vocabulary scribed for me on math tests because on one math quiz, Steve had to write for me. It was frustrating telling him exactly how to draw a square root symbol.

If you have never needed a note taker because you could not write, then you can consider yourself lucky. It took a little bit getting used to the other person's writing and their abbreviations before I could read everything they wrote. It is a lot harder to learn facts (i.e. a history class) when you are not the one writing the information down. Sometimes the note taker would not find the same things as important as I would. This was not the case for math as formulas and examples were written down, but in lecture classes I would tape record as well as get the notes from another person. It was hard to find time to listen to the taped lecture, but occasionally Mom would write something in my notes if I asked her.

(I was thankful for my note taker. I'm sure you're thankful for things that others take for granted. Think back on someone or something that you had to get help with because you could not accomplish them by yourself. Who helped you and how did they help you? I'd love to post your answers so that we can help others in appreciating the little things that we all sometimes take for granted. Send details to matt@mattschroeder.org or at my Facebook https://www.facebook.com/mattman419.)

The first quarter I just took that one math course. My Dad was very good at math, and he scribed for me on all my homework. He also tutored me and helped me with my daily writing of math assignments. My dad used this as an opportunity to refresh his math skills. During other quarters I randomly had Dad assist with writing, but other times it would get done at school in the math lab. Math tutors would help me when I had time to go.

My Grandma made me a red book bag that hung over the front of my walker, which was used for nearly my first two years of college. I could not maintain my balance without hanging on to something. Grandma did quality work with her sewing machine.

I became good friends with Donna Lamb, in the career services, and I would go there often. She remembered hearing about my automobile accident, mainly because I scored so well on the test to be a Buckeye scholar, and she was amazed to see me walking, although with a walker. I told her how neat the Ohio State clock looked hanging in her office. She told me it was mine if

I ever graduated. So I always reminded her of that whenever we crossed paths.

My parents, sister, and cousins were responsible for taking me to and from school and therapy that first year. I rode both to and from school on certain days during the winter and spring quarters of our inaugural year with my cousins, Clint and Kurt who also went to Lima campus for one year. Often times I only rode to school with them; on those days a family member picked me up from school and took me to outpatient therapy after class. Usually my cousins had three or four classes while I only had a part time course load. All three of us took an American History course together, and my cousin Clint even took notes for me in that class.

Despite my therapist's pessimistic warning, I did very well in my college experience. I received an A for that math class. My therapist's opinion was not a bad thing as nobody's opinions are right or wrong, except my own. She was going by what the general population's responses and results would be. Also, my situation was very extreme. Yet I could have allowed her pessimism to get me down and lose hope, or I could let it be just another reason to keep pushing forward.

(Sure there are people in your life who will be purposely pessimistic about you and something you're trying to accomplish. Then there will be people who mean well as they are trying to be realistic. See this as a chance to grow and filter what does or doesn't apply to you and see how you can grow from it. My therapist had good intentions. She just saw that there really wasn't too great of a chance that I would be able to do well in college, as most people wouldn't in my condition. Yet I'm not like

most people. In fact, I am my own unique self. And so are you. Be realistic, yet do not let that limit you in what you can do.)

It's About Time

Getting ready to be driven to OSU-Lima for the second day of my Math class in autumn, 1998.

The start of summertime was a much-needed break from school, but I still had outpatient rehabilitation so there was not a whole lot of relaxation going on. I was still operating with the extra four legs in order to be sure of my balance, and the left arm stayed fairly stationary against my body. My speech was still drawn out, but more people could understand me. Most of my classmates were either attending local colleges or were home for the summer. The problem was that I was unable to drive, and that limited the fun opportunities I had.

I was really getting sick of asking others to pick me up to go here or there, and it had been my thoughts for the last couple of months that I could handle driving just fine. The first step in order to drive was have a license, but I never had mine taken away. I knew not what the rules were regarding my driving and probably could have just driven a car out of our driveway and been legal, but I was a great guy who wanted to live by the spirit of the law, not just by its letters. I wanted to drive more so than the dry soil farmer wanted rain. I told my occupational therapist, Laura Schmeltzer, what I wanted to do, because I told her everything that was bothering me, but she was not in agreement with my ideas.

She informed me that the first thing I had to do to start the driving process was go through the simulator to see if my reaction times were up to par. She also said that I would not like to try it yet because if I failed, the wait would be three months before I could have another chance. Laura really thought my reaction times were too slow, and I would be unsuccessful in my attempt to prove her wrong. She did not realize how badly I wanted to try, and it was ludicrous to think anyone knows my thoughts or what I could do. My fate would be decided a few days later.

(Here I must mention that although you can set the direction and path for your life in many cases, there are still times where your fate will be decided without your control. Such as with my situation, I just had to wait for them to let me know. There was nothing I could really do to encourage or tweak what was yet to come. But I knew that whatever was to be determined,

111

I would make the best of it and see it for the challenge that it is to make me be better. I encourage this for you in your life as well.)

The simulator was in a room off the occupational therapy headquarters so I could not justify waiting three months if I was not successful. Maybe that was a made up story and maybe not, but either way, the pressure added suspense to the day. Later I learned that using the simulator was an expensive practice, and it was the health insurance provider that made me wait a quarter year before trying again if I had an unsuccessful attempt; that made more sense. It was an almost perfect day when I showed Drill Sergeant Schmeltzer what I could do. Even she was amazed that I did a passing score. Laura passed the information on to my doctor and I made an appointment to see her.

When I went to the neurologist's office, she set up a session with a driving evaluator, and if I was impressive with the driving evaluator, my doctor said she would recommend me for driving. I drove almost perfectly in my experience with the approved evaluator and was excited to meet with the neurologist. What transpired next made me wish that someone else with more people skills were the one making the call on whether or not I could start driving again. This head doctor tried to make me take another driving test with a different specialist in Columbus.

I was not going to be driving in a city, so to me that did not make sense. The closest I ever came to driving in a city was passing through Dayton on interstate. I guess Lima's population classifies it as a city and that is close to where I live , but there were no skyscrapers. I lived in rural area just outside of a small village and was not going to drive in densely populated areas with high traffic. The city drivers are of a different breed. Driving in

Columbus for another evaluation scared me because the results were sure to be different than in Putnam County.

I was upset and reminded the doctor that she specifically said she would recommend me for driving if I performed impressively with that evaluator. I was mad, and Dad let me fight my own battle. I could see going somewhere to retest if I needed some kind of adaptive equipment, but I drove a regular car with no irregularities so I argued my idea. The doctor was at a loss for words, and she approved my driving status. A big thing was that in the fall I would be able to drive myself to school and around other places too.

(For those of you who can relate to my frustration at having to deal with people who don't understand your vision and your abilities, focus on the positive reasons for why they don't understand. In my case, they wanted to make sure that I could handle what I so desperately longed for – for my sake and for the sake of others. My car accident was near fatal and as stated before, many would not have endured, survived, and recovered as I did. The doctor and therapists had good reasons to be concerned. Although, I wasn't happy about their pessimism and slow, careful ways to determine my capabilities since I was like a teenager waiting for his driver's license and the go-ahead to be more independent, I can see why they were so cautious.

To those of you who are driven and make success your goal, the ones who can innovate on a dime and make decisions and take actions very quickly, I encourage you to balance this drive with focusing on trying to understand and respect others' points of views. This will allow you to have more patience, see and appreciate others' uniqueness, gain from their input and feedback, and to make decisions that are based on well-rounded factors. This will help to reduce the natural tendency to be self-focused, frustrated, and impatient with others who don't move quite as fast as we do. And it reduces the chances of leaning towards arrogance, control freak, and impatience. Whether you change instantaneously or take what seems like a lifetime to make any changes, we are all human with a sinful nature that has to be balanced and controlled. We can learn from others as they can learn from us.)

A few afternoons per week in the summertime I would use my newly acquired driving skills to go to my Grandma Schroeder's house to do things with her. She was not like a stereotypical grandmother but was very energetic. We would occasionally visit people or grab something to eat. It never was to doubt though, that we usually ended up playing cards. Sometimes we did not go anywhere or do anything but play cards.

We played rummy or two-handed pinochle when it was only the two of us, but sometimes one of her kids would stop in, and we would play three handed. It did not matter what we played since both games were fun, and we each wanted to beat our opponent. Approximately one evening per week, Dad, some of his brothers, and I would play cards with Grandma. Most times we would play an old German game named Solo. That is a game Dad taught me and money is used, but the most anybody usually loses or wins is a dollar or two.

Driving seemed similar to being freed from the shackles of prison. (Never did I spend any time behind bars though.) Experiencing college life and not being able to drive was like tplaying golf without a ball. One can rehearse swinging clubs with no ball, but it lacks in fun. College became more bearable my second year even though I was not going part-time, but full time, due to being allowed to drive. I no longer had to burden my friends or family with a ride to school or therapy.

The question remained whether or not I would be too apprehensive to drive or get behind the wheel again. People were often amazed that I was not too timid to drive. Come on people! The only thing that I was worried about was that I would never be allowed to drive. It was an unwarranted feeling, as the thought had been about living in a hospital forever when in Dodd Hall. The only difference was that when I was in Columbus, I was utterly confused and things appeared in disarray, but when I was recovering from home, I was logically sound, but still worried daily about not driving. Both times I felt frustration, but soon I was able to operate an automobile.

Registering my car on the Ohio State University at Lima campus was a proud moment in my life. There was a large handicapped-parking section on the campus, which made traveling from car to class using a walker easier. However, it still took longer for me to get around than most people. Therefore, I did not have much time to stop and socialize between classes.

I talked slowly, and it took a while for me to get my point across. My voice was projected slowly, and surely it was not fun to hear, but it was deliberate and loud enough to understand nonetheless. People who did not know my situation regularly spoke loudly to me. I always fell into the trap that I created of telling them my story so they would understand that I was in a car wreck and was not stupid. I knew that it did not matter what other people thought about me, not one iota, but I still told them anyway.

The college environment was hectic and sometimes people did not have time to listen to me talk or tell stories since I spoke slowly. They would walk away, forever thinking that I was challenged. Whether they did not have the time to listen or just did not care is unknown to me. At times being treated that way could make me feel like I did not matter in the grand scheme of things, but rather than allowing myself to get bogged down with why people did not want to listen or take the time, I simply looked forward and focused on the people that do listen. I was treated differently not by faculty but by students. Maybe I was challenged by not catching all the nuances in conversations with others that prevented me from effectively communicating with them.

It is surprising to see how many people who did not need handicapped spots had handicapped placards and parked in the front row spaces. The same was true of restaurants or shopping facilities. When I went to out to eat or to go shopping, I did not use my handicapped sign, which hung from my rear view mirror when it was used, because there might have been someone in a wheelchair who really needed to park close. Although walking slowly with a walker gave me reason to use the closer parking, I left those spots for someone who needed them.

Driving was perhaps most advantageous when I left school three times per week my second year to go to rehabilitation. Across the street from Saint Rita's, the hospital had an outpatient therapy building where I worked to get better faster. There was even a walkway with glass walls connecting the rehabilitation building to the hospital. That was pretty neat, but I only used the enclosed tunnel a few times. A lot of time was spent in the therapy rooms as I continued with my occupational, speech, and physical therapies more at that time.

Getting Back

I didn't like speech therapy, and that's not because I didn't want to improve my speech. Speech therapy was frustrating for me because I worked so hard and yet barely noticed any positive results. I made improvements over time but did not necessarily recognize positive changes from speech therapy right off the bat. I would not have enough patience to be a speech therapist. The speed of my speech did increase somewhat, but I was never satisfied with my speech. Maybe that is what kept me striving toward improvements. It was difficult for me to recognize weekly improvements. It took a lot of patience to get comfortable with the speed at which the gradual changes took place. People encouraged me and told me how I had improved each week, but I did not see these changes. Maybe I was too critical of myself.

(Perfectionism. Are there times when you are too critical of yourself? It always seems valid striving to reach such a high plateau when it is one guarantee that no human is perfect, because even though you won't attain the goal you have a much greater chance of coming near it. Maintain a relentless attitude

in your effort to succeed in reaching those unattainable ideals, but be prepared to try new tactics, for failure is inevitable at times. I was never satisfied with anything I attempted if there was room to do better.

If you are not accustomed to building off of shortcomings in order to eventually reach success, possibly viewing things in a perfectionists' way is not a wise thing to do. Perhaps you will become frustrated, angry, or discouraged and that's not the ideal thing to do. Detrimental it would be if you forfeit major tasks because you are disgruntled by not reaching those high goals, that were self-set, and then you stop trying. You must start small and work your way up.)

Physical therapy made me feel like I was getting something done, and I practiced moving with the walker a lot. I met many new people in physical therapy. My real personality was starting to shine, and when I got to know new people, we often times joked around about anything and everything. One of my physical therapists, I think her name was Tina, was a huge University of Michigan fan. It was the start of football season, and we trash talked each other's favorite team when the opportunity arose, in a playful and friendly way.

Through all my various types of rehab, occupational therapy was the most fun, easy, and hardest all at the same time. That sounds impossible, but it is true. In OT Laura and I went swimming once per week, and I never actually was able to swim, but went in the pool. The hot tub was always the final sanctuary each swim day before we finished, and the warmth was so relaxing. We usually stayed on the shallow side, working with my left arm, but every pool day I begged to go in the deep section and never was given the chance. Remember that I grew up by the Columbus Grove swimming pool and was a fish out of water.

I remember one time, a while before therapy ended, we were in the water, and, as usual, I begged to go in the deep end. At last my request was granted, which seemed long overdue. (At the library when a book gets returned late, there is a fee charged, but what happened next was payment enough in this case.) Since I could not swim or tread water, Laura Schmeltzer went with me. She said that when I could do the task that she did, I would be done with therapy altogether. Those last four words seemed magical, and they triggered my full attention.

We were holding on to the edge of the pool. As I carefully watched, Drill Sergeant Laura pushed back with her feet and did a large circular backwards flip, resurfacing with her front facing the ledge in the same direction as she started. She looked so graceful. Then it was my turn to try the underwater flip and possibly end therapy, finally.   After what Laura said seemed like forever, I circled around and resurfaced while pumping my right fist in the air exclaiming that I was "done", although I knew that we weren't, nor did I really want to be done right then!

We did many unusual things that made occupational therapy the most enjoyable of all my rehabilitation. I had to do all kinds of intricate detail for Drill Sergeant, such as putting wooden pegs into a board or measuring ingredients to cook with. Doing things like that with my left hand was very hard, but it was not exhaustingly difficult like running a mile. It was much less tiring than physical therapy.

At the same time that I was making drastic improvements to my body, I was improving my mind too. Being a full time student was not all that easy. Difficulty in the classroom during the fall of 1999 was due partially to the material but mostly to my

119

instructor of psychology, I think. You see, I was taking fifteen credit hours, which was a lot for me.

I was determined as anyone to do well in college, and I had to work hard at it. That was where my past experiences bit me in the butt. High school was not difficult whatsoever, and I rarely did homework or studying at home. College was quite the opposite, and the challenges before me were only intensified due to not being able to take my own notes, and it was hard for me to get my work done on time. I could not get my assignments done at school for there were too many distractions. By that time, I had met many more people, and there were always people to talk with. I was not that good at multitasking.

The first couple of years I took one math class per quarter, or at least a class that involved math in some degree, because math came easily to me the second time around. I had forgotten formulas and methods to solve advanced math problems that I knew before the accident, but that information came back fairly easy to me too. I pushed as hard in school as I did during therapy. Math helped me maintain a decent grade point average, and I made the Dean's List on several occasions. However I did have classes that were undesirable and my grades suffered as result.

Time to Focus on Career

To walk in commencement ceremonies, from Ohio State, in the Shoe will never be forgotten. The most rewarding thing was that I was able to walk despite being told I would probably never walk again approximately five years earlier. It seemed ironic that it was Dodd Hall at the OSU Medical Facility where I was told that, and I graduated from that University, almost like I was proving them wrong.

Studying Elementary Education at Ohio State required that I get a Master's after my bachelor degree was attained. The Lima campus had the Master of Education program which seemed rather convenient. Initially, I was excited and had hopes about being a classroom teacher because that would give me ample opportunity to mold students' lives. Being a math or science instructor to middle school adolescents was the only pathway I saw to reach my goal. Approval from the faculty to be in Masters Program was sought and validated.

The one-year, actually five quarters, M.Ed. program had its difficulties, but success was in my cards, so I attacked the loaded schedule with optimism. I try to be an optimistic person in every situation, and I've never regretted any attempt made to improve my situation. My view for the longest time saw me positively influencing lives in the classroom, as a teacher. Putting forth effort is not a regrettable offense, never was nor will be.

Being a full-time graduate student, as compared to the same full load while pursuing an undergraduate degree, was like comparing night and day, respectively. The biggest problem for me was the large amounts of daily typing/writing that needed to be done. I worked and somewhat struggled through the summer reading program which kicked off the masters program, but made it through while maintaining the required grade point average for staying in the graduate degree program.

I was well versed on using a computer, but the slight tremors in my right hand made keyboarding difficult. That situation was very frustrating, because I knew where all the keys were, but my non-dominant hand was the only steady one when attempting intricate things. Everything took much longer to get down on paper and although sometimes I became angry when I couldn't do what I used to do, I chose to be thankful and make the best of it. All was okay. I was undeterred.

Then I completed my fall quarter. The classroom experience at a satellite middle school away from Lima was difficult along with the coursework and writing required for the master's agenda. I asked the instructor heading the program if I was cut out for teaching since the technicalities were becoming difficult to complete on time, but he reassured me that if I kept working, things would turn out roses.

The thunder of winter quarter was felt and hypothetical lightening struck me like I was holding a metal pole while walking through a thunderstorm. I was at a different classroom experience than the past quarter, and we were focusing on subject areas different from my concentration areas. Everyone in the program was required to follow this particular agenda, so I was not the only student who had a hard time accepting this assignment. I also knew this before the program started so it's not like they were veering from the laid out plan. It was rough with all the reading, writing, and lesson planning that needed to be completed outside the classroom for college courses. Through it all I worked at the requirements and was able to maintain the required grades.

At this point I was awaiting my placement for spring internship at yet a different school; this was to be the final in-the-classroom experience before becoming a traditional teacher. All of craziness of being a graduate degree student was nearing completion. Two days prior to the quarter starting, I had not gotten word about my placement, so I made a special trip to OSU-Lima campus to find out. The head person told me that the faculty decided not to recommend me for teaching, but offered me alternative Lima campus courses. If completed accordingly, I would still be awarded a M.Ed., just no teaching certification. With no obvious alternatives, I accepted, although feeling infuriated since this scenario came about after the entire program was paid for with money, countless time, and frustrations.

Anger quickly subsided as I decided that I was going to make the best of the situation. I probably could have fought the system and the University from a legal standpoint (as certain friends suggested), but I decided that a traditional classroom teacher just wasn't in His plans for me. Instead I determined that my education could be used to more greatly impact others' lives through speaking and helping others. I quickly lost the unjustified feeling that the program director was concerned solely that tuition was paid and not about helping me.

(Just as delicious lemonade is made out of a sour substance, so you, too, should focus on the positives in your life to transform negatives to positives. Wise choices were made on my part, and you too can make smart choices to work with current situations in your professional and personal life. I could have taken the legal route, and also let upsets fester until they got worse and worse, but I decided to work with what I had and make the best of it. Actually it turned out better as motivating and helping others is my passion.

When you step back and analyze any situation, know that there are people in your life offering guidance and support, but your actions are the ones that truly matter. Others' opinions and past should not be dismissed without hearing and may be used on occasion, but in the end know that everything is up to you. We are ultimately responsible for ourselves and hard work an effort is a small price to pay for success.)

Christopher Reeve
(Superman) and Me

Spinal cord injuries are life-changing events that can also bring lifestyles to abrupt halts. An enormous amount of time and work are spent to combat and try to improve injuries of this type. The organization that is most widely known for their work to help improve or find a cure for spinal cord injury is now called the Christopher and Dana Reeve Foundation. This foundation began as the American Paralysis Association, which formed in 1982. In 1995, after he joined and spearheaded much publicity and drove in many sponsors to fund much spinal cord research, the foundation embodied the sole name of Chris Reeve. Dana's name was added in 2011 to reflect the "partnership, courage and compassion of the Reeves." According to the Foundation, while Chris and Dana were still alive, they had been responsible for well over $70 million in combined research and quality of life grants, which improve the daily lives of people with paralysis.

Christopher Reeve was a world-renowned actor for the many characters he played in films, but was best known and often referred to by fans, as Clark Kent, Superman. He and I had similar injuries. He had broken two vertebrae in his neck after falling off a horse while pursuing equestrian activities in his spare time. Chris completed a last minute registration to be in a cross- country equestrian event that wasn't too terribly difficult. It may be coincidence, but it seems that last minute or split second decisions are frequently mentioned along with accidents or mistakes.

(A suggestion I have for you is, take your time and prepare for what lies in front of you. Last minute decisions rarely yield the best results, but it's a Catch 22 because being adaptive and able to make spur of the moment changes is occasionally essential for success. If you practice and really know what you are doing, catastrophic happenings become less likely. Accidents happen randomly though and cannot be practiced for. Instead give thanks, trust, and lean on God, and He will lead you through life essentially unscathed.)

At the age of 33, Christopher began horseback riding, and less than five years later, by 1989, he was competing in events, which included cross-country jumping. Reeve was having a good time while on vacation with his family in Virginia, and Chris loved riding horses for show. He walked through the course that he would ride in that weekend and wasn't concerned about any of the jumps except two near the end. But he never even made it to the course. The third and last practice jump, aimed to have his horse Buck ready for the event, turned out to be his final equestrian maneuver. Buck must have been startled by something, because he made a "dirty stop" right before the fence he was supposed to clear.

Superman toppled over the front of his horse, and his arms were slow getting out of the reins. Therefore, Christopher had no arms to lessen the impact when his head hit the ground. Reeve was wearing a helmet, though, and at least that protective device prevented any brain damage. As I've read Christopher Reeve's two autobiographies, I have to grin when I recollect about the similarities between our recoveries. Although Christopher Reeve was treated as a top shelf product wherever he went since he was a celebrity, I can relate with most of his happenings: his descriptions of getting acquainted with new hospitals, vent tubes coming off, and seeing humor in a lot of things. However, his unwillingness to accept what happened to himself, vulgar language, and view on God, were alarmingly different from me.

(A side note for your life application: Depression is common among people with severe injuries. Family can often be the anchor to help you raise your spirits. I am blessed to have family and friends with the similar go-getter attitude that I have. Family should be your first priority and the most important thing to hold close.)

Reeve's second book after his equestrian mishap, <u>Nothing Is Impossible,</u> reinforced non-similarities between us come like a locomotive in a quiet and serene setting. He continued to reject the reality of what had happened to him. Like in Hollywood blockbusters, the first movie is typically the best one if there are sequels. I can feel like I'm there while reading his first book, <u>Still Me</u>, but the sequel lost that dramatic affect on me. The best way to understand a person is to actually meet them face-to-face, though.

A lightning bolt struck about four weeks prior to my bachelor degree commencement ceremony. The lightening strike was while driving my car to OSU-Lima campus on a warm May morning, and it was about as real as there is seventy minutes in an hour. This hypothetical lightning strike was when I heard on the radio, while driving to Lima campus, that Christopher Reeve was going to be the commencement speaker at the Ohio State University in the spring. I was scheduled to graduate when he was speaking! I was super excited but maintained my sanity long enough to get to school safely.

Once there I rushed to the Public Service buildings to talk to somebody about calling down to Columbus and maybe setting up a meeting between Chris and me, but I quickly learned that that was not going to happen. My advisor was busy, yet I did speak with Wayne Kaufman who was also an advisor, and a friend to me. He was not very computer savvy, but I convinced him to look up the Reeve Foundation's telephone number. We did and called them, and what happened next was detrimental to my excitement.

After speaking with Colleen at the foundation, who initially took down my contact information as a common courtesy, for about 45 minutes, telling my story, and practically begging to meet Christopher, she told me that I had a tremendous story.

Unfortunately, she received many requests daily from people who wanted to meet Chris for this or that reason. Then she closed, expressing sorrow that I would not get to meet him. I did feel sorry that my efforts went by the wayside. I thought I had lost the battle, but there could be another way to win the war. I'd keep trying.

In the afternoon when my classes were over, I made it over to the Career Services department, also in the Public Service building. Donna Lamb, my friend and worker there would be able to think of another way to meet Superman while we were both on OSU's main campus in Columbus, I hoped. Donna called a contact on main campus, but they were just going to check on that. I made an effort to connect with the big time actor, tried my best (that's integral to personal success,) but was not enthused about the results. In sports people can win some with a strong effort, and other times they will score worse than the other team. Teams, similarly to individual performers, will be successful if certain goals were met. It appeared to be an unsuccessful try to meet Reeve, but I had met my goal because I had done everything I could to set up an encounter.

The weekend passed and Monday morning the phone rang; the sound of lightening striking would have been more fitting, but it was the traditional landline ring. I answered and surprisingly, it was Colleen from the Foundation! She said not to get all excited for I was not going to meet Chris Reeve, but they did have a meeting at the foundation in New York or New Jersey, and they decided, as a group, to send my story on to Chris in Texas. Furthermore, they said Chris would send me his two autobiographies, a dictated letter, and a large picture of himself.

Well, I thought, at least I was going to receive those things from Christopher Reeve, and I had put forth my best effort.

Let me jump ahead three weeks now to the week when all graduates must go to the main campus for practice the morning before the big ceremony which was to be on Friday June 13, 2003. It was Monday and the phone rang. It turned out to be the Director of Student activities at the Ohio State University main campus. She said she had received an unusual request for me to meet and greet Christopher Reeve the night before commencement during the invitation-only party at the Blackwell Inn in Columbus, right on campus. She called to give me a few days to adjust my schedule and see whether or not I could make it. Of course I replied affirmatively but asked what was so unusual about that because I was trying to set the meeting up for about three weeks. She said it was a rarity because Christopher Reeve called Ohio State and requested me.

I couldn't believe it, but my call to the foundation must have worked. The only people who had an opportunity to meet and talk to him the night before graduation were Karen Holbrook, the then-president of the University, the four student government officers, and me. When the day came, we were instructed by Superman's Public Relations people to get in a single file line and then just tell him our name, the office we held, and the degree we were getting. Karen Holbrook went first and said her short intro to the university, then the student president, vice president, treasurer, and secretary went and said their info. All the while, I was slowly inching closer to the front of the line as people introduced themselves. The person directly in front of me finished. It was my turn, and I didn't know exactly what to say.

In reality, I must have stood there for almost a full second, and there was no sound from either of us, but it seemed and felt like an hour. Trust me, when my turn comes to talk, I typically have something to say. Christopher Reeve broke the ice by saying, "Oh, this must be Matt Schroeder, who I have been waiting to hear from." An outsider might say that's like opening a can of worms, and I immediately felt at ease sharing a short story of my accident and recovery. When I was almost finished, Chris inquired of me whether or not he could ask me a question. I knew my allotted time had already expired, but this was his time and his question so I replied with a "sure".

(A note to readers: I am not one to ever shy away from questions for I want to help people and if I'm ever not there to answer our question in person, please do not hesitate to send me an email message, matt@mattschroeder.org. You can also find me on Face book, www.facebook.com/mattman419.)

Giving Superman Advice

Superman asked me how I did it, how did I walk again. He was curious to know what I had done to get out of the wheelchair and regain the ability to walk again. I mulled it over in my head for a few seconds before telling him my response, which came from the heart. I said that it took a lot of hard work in therapy, much family support, and a ton of prayer. If violence were in my repertoire, I would have slapped myself because even though my response was accurate and my recovery took all those things, I knew from reading about Mr. Reeve that he questioned the goodness of and possibly even the existence of God in his first book, Still Me. He was kind of mad at the world and at God because of what had happened to him. He had not accepted what happened to him for a while after his accident. On the other hand, I never was angry with Him but always thanked God for letting me live and for the good things and family in my life.

Being well known globally as an actor and being wealthy probably contributed to the initial stalemate on improvement. Christopher may have been so used to people doing things for him that he was not familiar with doing tough tasks for his own self.

Maybe Reeve was so used to having enough money to buy his way out of trouble, that working hard to reach goals and move closer to his big goal, one step at a time, was foreign. My feeling about his fame and wealth is speculative, because I cannot relate with that kind of lifestyle, as far as large sums of money goes. A guess is the best that I can do.

In essence I responded truthfully but without careful thinking. I needed to find a way that made sense to Chris. Having somebody of Superman's status asking me about walking, seemingly to gain an insight for use in his own life, blew my mind. Christopher Reeve was obviously very interested in what little me had to say.

(No matter your situation, there are good and positive attributes in every situation. For instance, as much as I did love sports, basketball the most, there were more strains, pains, or injuries attained from practice or games. And that was a positive attribute in what could have been such a grim situation. Life is full of choices and in making the choice to focus on the truth — there are positive attributes in every situation- you will be able to see, live, and act on these truths. Thus recognizing these brings balance, and you'll have that a great feeling of accomplishment.)

Now back to the moment when I was answering Chris' questions. My encounter with Christopher Reeve is a prime example of relying on faith here, but never is my intention to challenge someone's religious beliefs if they are different from my own Catholic beliefs. Therefore, I avoided that response and answered the inquiry with a question of my own. I basically asked Chris if he thought **he** would ever walk unassisted again.

133

Superman looked me in the in the eyes, and almost immediately recited a short litany of things that if happened, doctors said might enable him to walk. My own opinion, after being told one thing by therapists and learning doctors' negative prognosis while still wheelchair-bound, is that the only one who really knows what one can do is often seen in the mirror. Everybody is entitled to his or her own opinions, and some may come from greater knowledge sources or after more schooling. A doctor or professional who is better educated may give a worthwhile hypothesis, but personal determination is worth nothing less. Well, God knows too, but only an individual knows what can be accomplished when he works at it. You can listen to others, but don't accept others' limitations for you unless they paint the same picture as seen by you. That was the difference between my successful recovery and his; I was able to accept and recognize my situation as real from the very beginning. Nobody but you knows what you physically can and cannot do, and even you cannot tell at times unless you try time and again. So I restated my question, asking him again if *he* thought he would ever walk again unassisted.

Chris said, "Yeah," but I felt a bit leery about his response until he commented about the scar on the back of my neck that looked exactly like his. Then I could see it in Reeve's eyes that I had gotten through to him. I am sure Christopher had the best help money could buy, and he did take about a half dozen steps, unassisted, before he passed away around 18 months after we met due to complication from surgeries. I do feel that encounter with me helped him. I hope that it did. If you were seriously injured and met someone who had a similar injury to you, only they had had a tremendous recovery, I think that would help you to have a little bit of hope. Please understand that I'm not taking anything away from his therapists, for I know therapists put forth great effort and do tremendous work, but little reassurances from someone who's been down that road always helps.

If something unfortunate or awful happens in life, it may seem that an individual's actions are irrelevant, but where that person goes from there depends upon the result of their efforts. Sylvester Stallone has a line in the Rocky Balboa movie where he is talking to his son about life and says, "The world ain't all sunshine and rainbows," and I agree with that statement. The character's life revolves around the ring, but oddly enough, the occasionally clueless Rocky character makes sense. He further tells his offspring that life is not about how hard you hit but rather how hard you can get hit yet still move forward. That comes from a boxer to his son, but one doesn't have to be a fighter to appreciate Balboa's words.

(Violence is not my forte so I'll shift back to how to deal with the bad happening example. There are several different thoughts of ways to deal with problems. Sometimes people have a difficult time accepting reality when a catastrophic event occurs. Instead they remain in denial, and often times they waste their time being depressed instead of working to improve their situation. Stay upbeat and focus on the positive.

Whether you are religious or not, God will assist in getting you through every difficulty encountered. He may send you physical or mental help and sometimes both, and He holds no grudges. God's already counts on your hard work, so try your best, relying solely on Him for everything. Not trying is a huge mistake. Always have faith and trust that God's ways are best.)

When Christopher asked me how I learned to walk, I knew that what I said at least had him thinking, because despite the fact that I already exceeded my allotted time, he only added to the talk by being inquisitive. His people had instructed the student government and me that Superman had to give a talk yet that Thursday evening over at the Ohio State University's medical facility, Dodd Hall. (Ironically, that is where I spent the largest amount of time when comatose.)

I never asked Reeve whether or not he had ever accepted his situation as a gift from God or whether he was still in denial, because it was neither the time nor place for that kind of inquisition. My online research since our encounter has led me to believe that he did accept the Lord before our conversation, but network research is not worthy of being classified as factual. The only certainty was to ask a direct question, but I already exceeded my allotted time limit so it was left unanswered.

Mr. Reeve had looked at the scar on my neck and said that it looked exactly like his scar. Wow! After hearing me and commenting on the similarity of our scars, a person has to believe that what I said made a difference in his life. He had tons of professional and outside help, the best money could buy, undoubtedly, but there is a small piece of me that feels our speaking together and tangibly seeing each other helped him improve. The iconic Reeve took around five continuous steps, unassisted, before he passed away.

(Having stated all of this, practical applications for real life must be applied. For example, if you are ever dealt a difficult situation and remain in denial, in depression, not accepting what life has thrown your way, please know that people can grow from their own situation. We can make things easier on ourselves

if we simply accept what happened as real and try to improve as soon as we can. Understand that His ways are best! God can help us through hard times if you give Him a chance, and God never gives you what you cannot handle. You are bound to make mistakes and fail, but failure is the first step to success next time. Your aim should always be to move forward.

Take your tough task and break it down into several smaller mini goals. That way you can easily reach smaller goals, and before you know it, you will have conquered the main task. And please do not be afraid to fail because you can usually try again. A few people will argue, logically that you cannot truly succeed until you fail. My opinion is that you can never fail as long as you keep trying. You may not finish with more points or a better score, but you will be a winner. That goes for all things in life, not just sports, and the only true losers are those who pack it in, giving up.

I admire Christopher Reeve's will and desire to help find a way to reduce people's problems with the spinal cord and paralysis. He is a hero to many people for what he had championed through. I'll never forget the time that I got to spend with him.

It's okay to have your hero as someone in reality or a family member or friend. Often times, when asked who our heroes are, many people feel pressured to say someone famous or mention some iconic character. The reasons may be due to thinking that we should announce someone famous or perhaps we don't really want to or think of who really deserves the credit of being our true hero. Give the person who truly has made you who you are the title of being your hero.)

Issues

Issues, some possibly stemming from the fateful day in 1997, randomly made themselves evident in my life, while others had no known ties to my wreck. Some included issues and re-issues with my knee due to a basketball injury. The car accident had left me with a rod inserted at my hip that filled the left leg's femur bone. My diaphragm along with other internal parts had been put back in place and reattached. My spleen did not survive the storm that had made a direct hit within me. I have a small metal plate in my head and titanium pins that fuse two vertebrae together in my neck. Most of these had lain dormant for years with few problems.

For years I had had a bit of a protein spill into my urine, and several doctors told me that was acceptable for my body, because it remained at a constant for 11 years. However, trouble was brewing fairly severely during the summer of 2008. Luckily I went to a free kidney screening. My blood pressure was extraordinarily high, and I had been having a terrible headache for a few days. The end result of having terrible head pains coupled with abnormally escalated reading from the blood pressure cuff sent me in the hospital for two nights and three days. I began taking medication and water pills for nearly a year. It is uncertain whether that medical episode was related to later kidney issues, but the writing was spray painted on the wall, nonetheless.

Turning thirty in May 2009 began a nightmare, but after I awakened from one night's rest, the frightening dream did not end. My legs became swollen and sore, and I was becoming extremely winded and exhausted when doing the slightest physical activity. By the beginning of June my whole body was growing enormous, not just my legs, and I was taking a maximum dosage of prescribed pain medication to help ease my throbbing headache. To top everything off, I constantly had to find a restroom as my bladder constantly felt like it needed to be emptied.

This decline in my health called for an emergency appointment with Dr. Moser, a Lima nephrologist. I was astonished when I tipped the scales at 239 pounds when weighing in before the appointment. The nephrologist suspected some allergic reaction leading to renal failure, and the disappointing thing was that this specialist frowned upon water pills. Dr. Moser said they were only making things worse. Because of kidney failure, fluid began to infiltrate my body, and my clothes all seemed to be shrinking. Sweatpants were the only pants I was able to fit into. Even though minor swelling existed in my left leg since high school, now both legs became enlarged. My appearance was not of somebody who was in quality shape. Something was definitely in disarray with my body, and it needed to be fixed.

It was one problem after the other. Then scarring showed up on my kidney walls, and the diagnosis pointed to kidney failure. Talk about extreme frustration and stressors on every level! This failure of kidneys is not something to be taken lightly. Dialysis was begun, and I eventually would need a kidney transplant.

Dialysis is horrible to say it nicely! A tube was surgically inserted into my chest in order to hook to the machine that removed liquid from my blood. Every time infection set in at the tube insertion point, another surgical procedure to reinsert the tube in a new location was required. A clear plastic tube, which was used to remove water from my body, jutted out of my chest making me feel like a Thanksgiving feast. A turkey is typically stuck with a baking thermometer to see if the insides are done, and if it were November assuredly that's how I would have felt. Luckily it was only the start of autumn, but that meant the beginning of football season for a sports minded person such as me.

My diet was the biggest problem creator, though. It was very restrictive as to what and how much I could eat or drink when I was on kidney dialysis. I usually had my favorite, pizza, weekly before my kidney issues, but I did not have pizza for months, the entire time I was on dialysis. It may have been only about five or six months, but it seemed like an eternity. Following a renal diet with restrictive fluid intake was more difficult than it sounded. It put a big damper on my day. Having machine-assisted kidney function did a number on me, and each session made me feel very tired and worn out. Watching paint dry was as fun and interesting as sitting in the clinic three days per week.

The process of dialysis itself was painful, too. The machine functioned as my kidneys would if they were in working order. The whole time I sat in the same chair and randomly cramped up. Then when the four hours of boredom was nearing completion, I might reach what is called my dry weight, in other words, my bloodstream had no more excess water in it. I felt excruciating pain in my legs as they approached their dry weight. Sometimes 10-15 pounds were lost at dialysis, but it was not some wonder diet scheme as the water weight was put back on before the next session.

Several minor surgical tube reinsertion procedures occurred before doctors finally inserted a fistula, a tube connected to an artery in my left arm. That meant no more tubes sticking out of my chest - yippee! Gaining an easier access location for dialysis had its favorable points, but a major pitfall, too. This fistula eliminated infections as well as the precautions about having the chest tube tugged on which could start it bleeding, but it also hinted at longer-term dialysis.

Now I needed a kidney transplant. Dealing with this on top of making up for any inadequacies from my car wreck was a difficult adjustment to make. However I know that God will not deal you what you cannot handle. I had ample time to think about everything while doing dialysis, and that is what I did, albeit there was plenty of pain at these sessions. So I chose not to let anger, frustration, and other negative emotions and feelings take over. I must admit this wasn't always easy.

Fortunately, transplants were becoming more frequent than in the past, and my loving parents helped me cope. There was a night early on where tears were shed. I'm not ashamed to admit that either, because I know that crying is a good way to vent your frustrations. Everything was getting to me as far as the accident, kidney failure, and dialysis goes. My life was altered big time and my diet, while using machines as kidneys, was practically unbearable. Fluid intake remained very limited, as well as fruits, proteins, and potassium, and sodium (salt) was not consumed at all. While on dialysis my restrictive diet almost completely eliminated peanut butter, which had been practically a staple in my life. I had to find a focus other than the pain and suffering although I knew life's challenges make you stronger. At times when most things are going against you, it's equally important to find the small positives in your work, as it is to do the work. So I focused on Jeremy Schnipke who was, in essence, in charge at the clinic where I went three days per week. He is a friend I never would have met without kidney failure.

"When can I get a kidney?" I asked my RN Jeremy, sounding much too much like a child on Christmas morning. I was becoming impatient and frustrated, having to endure nearly 15 hours per week devoted to dialysis. "It will take only 4-6 months once you are on the donor list if you are lucky," he responded. So much for all the childlike excitement. From Jeremy's words, the timetable to get a transplant seemed unbearable.

Receiving a kidney is a slow process and isn't a sure-fire deal in many situations. First, either a living donor or a cadaver match had to be found in order for a transplant to be possible. Dialysis had to continue three times per week, five-hour sessions, until a matching kidney was found. I was blessed because I had a living donor which greatly sped up the wait. My four-years-older-than-I cousin, Ben Schroeder, volunteered one of his kidneys because we have the same blood type. But there was much testing that had to be completed to make sure the donor and recipient were close enough tissue matches to move forward with transplant.

I had several more friends and relatives, who also had type O blood, who wanted to help me out, but they were just there for backup. First the University of Cincinnati was checking to see if Ben was a match. If my relative produced a match in blood type, tissue matching and further tests would take around four months, and to me that seemed like an eternity. Everything medically speaking seems to take a long time.

I felt blessed to have a prospective donor because giving a donor organ of any kind is a selfless act. The estimated wait for a transplant, coupled with the age of the patients next to me at dialysis, I honestly thought I'd be having dialysis for a very long time. It sounds quite harsh, but I felt dying in the clinic was a possibility. Professionals always prepare you for the worst possible outcome. A child feels lost and scared when they are separated from their parents or guardians at a huge place like Cedar Point, and that's how I felt as weeks passed by, and I was still receiving mechanical kidney function. Well, simply scared, not lost.

However, a week or two after getting my fistula, my cousin Ben was approved as a match. My thinking was that the transplant would happen a week after confirmation that Ben was a match. When my pre-kidney transplant coordinator, Ashley Herzog called to say Ben was a valid donor, she had rather disappointing news as well. The doctors wanted to remove my kidneys about four weeks before they did the transplant, and that was not welcome news, but it was not completely detrimental either. Here is my blog entry on September 18, 2009:

Yesterday afternoon I received a call from Ashley Herzog, the transplant coordinator at the University of Cincinnati. That is where I am having my procedure done. My cousin sent his blood work in over two weeks ago but we finally got word that his blood was close to mine that he will be able to donate one of his kidneys to me. There are still tests that need to done and Ashley told me that I'll likely have a new kidney in about a month. That instantly makes dialysis not quite so bad. Now I am confident that it will end in the near future. You also know that means only four weeks remaining of limiting my fluids and following this strict diet. Woohoo!

Holding My Breath

University hospital in Cincinnati was my choice for transplant, and the removal was to be done there, too. Three days was what the doctors forecast as the length of my hospital stay for this procedure. How nice that would have been.

Surgery to remove my kidneys was scheduled for October 23, and sometime before that, I made a journey to Cincinnati where I met Dr. Tevar, who would be doing the removal. When he came into the room, we instantly connected. This guy appeared to be about my age or younger, and he was wearing a Chicago Bears bandana on his head. Remember, I'm not a shy person when I meet somebody new, and I love to talk. A bit more than a week after the removal of my kidneys, the Chicago Bears were scheduled to play at Paul Brown Stadium against the Cincinnati Bengals. Of course I am a Bengals fan, so indeed fun was had with the surgeon. All the guys on my Dad's side had arranged tickets for the game, and I wasn't going to be able to make it, said the doctor. It was very disappointing, but going to the game was nothing life or death either. My health was important to me, and still is!

Rather than take in the atmosphere of the NFL football game, I made a bet with Dr. Tevar on the outcome of the clash between the two teams which fulfilled my competitive spirit. If the Bears won, I had to tape a note that read, "I love the Bears" on the front of my hospital gown after my transplant surgery, and if the Bengals won, he had to get his picture taken with me while wearing a Bengals hat.

Meeting Dr. Tevar had me feeling not so worried about the kidney ordeal, and the fact that he joked around a lot and was a sports enthusiast made my next week of dialysis prior to surgery seem to go faster. His witty comments made me feel like I was right at home, and if only his words were considered, this doctor seemed like an uncle. That's partially why I believe humor is one of the best medicines to treat all kinds of illnesses. Prayer and laughter both fit any budget, too

On the same day of the removal of my kidney, there was a conflict with the hospital, and no room would be available for a while afterwards. After surgery I went to the post-anesthesia care unit where I was supposed to be for around an hour until the anesthesia subsided. I woke up, but the University had over-booked patient rooms. To put it differently, there was no room in the inn for me. Instead, remain in the PACU for 30 hours, I did.

My sister, an RN at a different hospital in Cincinnati, informed our parents that not moving me to the kidney floor for such a long time might be detrimental. Lisa said I needed one nurse assigned to me who was familiar with caring for renal patients. Later the next afternoon, everything started to feel strange, a little bit surreal perhaps. It was an oddity that was thought to be part of the recovery process. This was my first major

146

surgery since my accident, and medical staff thought that my body was having a hard time adjusting to anesthesia.

Later that evening I began hallucinating. I was watching the Buckeyes play football in a game and on a T.V. (while neither existed). I also remember vividly lying near the stairs in a kitchen and watching my two dead uncles playing cards with my aunt Ginny up on the second story of a two story complex. Reality was that the room I was in was just a plain one-story hospital room. And everything clearly was not OK, because out of everybody I know, Aunt Ginny would be the last one ever found playing cards for enjoyment. That second night of my hospital stay I slept little, as is the case for any hospital stay with beeps, lights, and readings being checked for this or that, leaving little peace and quiet for shut eye, but I recall little of those distractions.

Rather I was seeing relatives and friends playing baseball on my wall. They all had larger than life features such as heads and arms, and players on my team were randomly being decapitated. Sounds odd, that's understood. It too was accounted for by a bad reaction to anesthesia. I was planning to go home on that third day, and everyone thought things would go smoother in my normal setting at home.

After lunch on the third day at University hospital I went on a walk down the hallway. Physicians already determined my bowels would start working again soon although they had not yet. What happened next was a blessing in disguise.

I was still very weak, although I had been up, walking around, but I still needed help with most things. Dad was assisting me getting showered and cleaned up to go home. I passed out just before getting wet in the shower, and I coded. That was the second time I had coded in my life. Remember I coded once the night after my car wreck. In came the doctor, in came the nurse, and in came the lady with the alligator purse. Wait that's a nursery rhyme, and I don't know what that "coding" entails, but I have been told that it is a life-threatening situation that needs immediate medical attention.

I recall everything up to the second before passing out, and what I did recall did seem too weird. The visions I had been having were more than side effects of surgery. I remember bits and pieces of the next five days and most of the following four. That's right, what was supposed to be two nights quickly turned into 12 days. My sister must have known what she was talking about.

I had a blocked bowel. Any detailed memories from the next five or six days are permanently absent, but when I came to my senses, something on my face seemed severely wrong. There was a tiny tube called a nasogastric (NG) tube through my nose and down into my stomach. The tube removed fluids and gas and helped relieve pain. It would have been tolerable had I been able to eat or drink, but the tube was giving my body a chance to relax and heal.

Although I have no recollection or specific knowledge of my helpers prior to coding, the Physician Assistants (PAs) associated with me deserve large awards and high acclaim. I think her sidekick's name was Kara, but Kassia was the most important person aiding in my recovery. We had longer discussions, were similar in age, and aside from my loving family and a few friend visits, Kassia Knudson was my connection to the world. Although this hospital stay lasted only 12 days, it seemed like longer and I appreciated having the extra attention from this staff member.

After my NG tube was out for a few days, I had permission to eat pizza. My past associations with and great appreciation of pizza was made apparent to Kassia, in one of our chats between her busy schedule, and she brought some no- hospital- food- pizza in my room for lunch once before I was released. I would like to see her again sometime.

(Keep your eyes on the goal, and try not to let circumstances away from the task-at-hand make an impact in the outcome of the task-at-hand. Using football in example, notice how the things a receiver does correlates well with what the average person desires or expects in life. A multitude of positions on a football team are responsible for catching the football so everybody should get familiar and be ready to grasp the ball in case it comes your way. In the same way, something drastic occasionally does happen to you, being ready to advance in all stages of living seems proper.)

Kidney Transplant

When I went back home with no kidneys, I had dialysis for about a week and a half before transplant surgery time. Believe me, I disliked, and maybe even, detested it, more than prior experiences, but I knew that I was on the home stretch. I like to keep my goal in focus.

The most weird and occasionally beneficial thing about having no kidneys was the fact that I did not worry about finding a restroom to empty fluids from my body. Having complete absence of kidneys meant no urination.. One would think that would be advantageous when traveling and such, which it was, but the only place I went in the automobile was to and from the clinic three times per week and to church on Sunday. The most hated trait of dialysis before removal was diet and fluid intake restrictions; at least I had a little kidney function back then. But when my kidneys underwent a Houdini trick and disappeared, rather were surgically removed, my dietary guidelines took an even bigger toll on my morale. A smaller amount of fluid intake was allowed, and the only solace was I only had to endure this artificial kidney function for a little more than a week before experiencing the real thing again.

November 18 was the scheduled day my cousin would so selflessly give me one of his kidneys. Ben and I will always be cousins, but we made the jump to be also forever unique family members: kidney- brothers. There was much worrying done, and apprehension about surgery is fairly common, but I was worried about the health of the donor <u>and</u> me. If one of us became sick, it would postpone the switch which would mean more dialysis. The best way to cope when experiencing fear is with prayer. Asking God for help is imperative in every situation, and that mentality started as a seed in my adolescence and has grown into a young tree.

Prayers from everybody were appreciated, and the transplantation happened when planned, November 18, 2009. Dr. Woodle was my transplant surgeon, and in a surgical room just down the hall from where my transplant would happen, Dr. Tevar was going to be removing Ben's kidney just before it was to be adopted and become mine. Remember about Dr. Tevar's bet with me? I sure remembered, but the doctor had never taken a picture wearing a Bengals hat, even though the Bengals had experienced a lopsided victory. I like to talk, and when the transplant surgeon asked me if I had any further concerns, I shared the story of the unfulfilled bet with him. Luckily Dr. Woodle was a sports-minded and humorous guy like me, because he made some calls, received a hat from his aunt, and pulled Dr. Tevar over to take the picture with me moments before rolling me into surgery. It may have been last minute and I had surgery on my mind but, as you can see in my picture at the end of this section, I had a hilarious time.

When they transferred me to the surgery table and gave me an extra dose of happy gas, the last thing I remember doing was giving Dr. Woodle the hand signal and saying, "Hook'em Horns." During a pre-op appointment with the surgeon, I learned he did his undergraduate studies at the University of Texas and was a sports fanatic. I researched and found that greeting, "Hook'em Horns" and a special hand signal was a common one for alumni of the university. Even though I was a true and thorough fan of my alma mater (OSU), I figured that making the guy feel at home who was doing the surgery that my life hinged upon couldn't hurt. Dr. Woodle surely felt comfortable as he did transplants often, and the comment was more or less a reassurance that everything I could do was done.

"Look at that all that urine just shooting out of there," is the next thing I heard. It was after my surgery and the nurses were talking among each other. Later that November day, after I came to my senses, my parents told me of the great success of the transplant and everyone was happy. That first night was a little rough as I was having trouble adjusting to the room temperature. First I would be too cold, and then I would be too warm. Rejection was somewhat typical, and I got all bent out of shape about it, but by morning things were going well. Christine and her mom came to see me in the morning which was awesome, but they paled in comparison to my next visitor.

Previously I had mentioned one of my Physician Assistants, Kassia, who became a friend and served as a liason between the real world and hospital life when my kidneys were removed. Kassia brightened my day soon after the transplant, too. She cared enough about my condition to come and visit me after I got my new kidney. One thing is certain; surely my look was much healthier without a tube running out my nose! My spirits were lifted too, and we went on a short walk, but the longest I'd taken since transplantation, with her. Although Kassia still worked at University hospital for a while, I was not anxious for another renal episode to see her. At the present, she is married, living and working overseas. They may relocate to Cincinnati some day, and I would love to see her again because it is nice to stay in contact with someone who had such an impact on my life.

A room on the kidney floor was available this go-round at the hospital, and judging by workers who dealt with me this time, I surmised they were all made aware of my poor experience with University hospital a month earlier. Maybe my blocked bowel after the removal held some clout, or maybe having people familiar with renal care helped contribute to what I considered top of the line treatment. As I chose where to sign up for a transplant, I found that The University of Cincinnati was rated as the best place in the nation to receive kidney transplants.

The projected stay after removal had been three days which catapulted to 12 days with the obstruction. After the Wednesday morning transplant, medical staff figured that a release would happen Monday morning of the next week. A meeting between my surgeon, other doctors, nurses, post kidney transplant coordinator, and my Dad and me was held in my hospital room on Friday afternoon to determine when a dismissal would occur. This discussion was of importance to me.

I had been hearing from my drainage tube doctor, (I had monitors, wires, and tubes everywhere,) other doctors, my coordinator and various nurses that Dr. Woodle had been sharing about me in conferences. He told of my miraculous recovery from a heinous auto crash, how big of an Ohio State fan I was, and about the picture he took with his i-phone© of Dr. Tevar, wearing a Bengals hat, and me.   People told me that Dr. Woodle never talked and smiled so much when mentioning his other patients as with me. I had a grand time discussing football with him too, but this meeting about my dismissal was of great importance.

I would be released early the next morning. Only three nights after transplant surgery was almost unheard of then, and I was a little apprehensive. For once in my life I was actually looking forward to being in the hospital that Saturday afternoon. They told me I could leave later in the day if I'd rather. I didn't want to leave until the afternoon because, you see, this was no ordinary, run-of-the-mill Saturday; it was an Ohio State vs. Michigan football afternoon. It was a day that most of the college football world was aware of, and every Ohio State fan was aware of.

Joe, a friend who had been a volunteer with me at St. Rita's hospital in Lima, was even planning a trip to see and watch the game with me on the giant-sized television that covered most of the wall in my hospital room. That was the plan, and I was looking forward to watching the rivalry on the humongous TV. So Joe came on his motorcycle, brought Subway for lunch, and Dad and I enjoyed the game with him. Then we waited for the whole checkout process, which is slower than expected in every hospital, and we were off to my sister's by early evening.

(It's important to stay up beat and positive in any situation in the tree of life. Things will not always unfold as you plan and other times they may give you a hopeless or useless feeling, but if you can see where you want to be, go for it. Even when you don't reach the apex of the task at hand, not even as high as the competition, you will still win if you do the best you

154

can. A perfect way for me to do that is with humor, and maybe that will work for you too. It gives your mind a rest from painful thoughts or worrying about everything else, and being light hearted in your approach on everything and viewing things with a witty perspective is usually free, too. It's always wise to trust God, and our Creator never intended for us to be serious all the time, or else we wouldn't have the ability to smile or laugh.)

The Rest is Up to You!

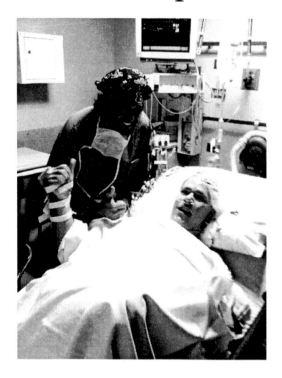

Dr. Tevar fulfilling the terms of the bet he lost. I am getting ready for transplant well after our bet had been determined, but better late than never!

The easiest way to get past something unpleasant that has happened is to move forward. You can't change it, nor should you look back. Events happened for a reason and now it's time to move on.

You need to forgive and be at peace with others, and yourself, and, most importantly, with God, because, with forgiveness, comes your shining moment. Be kind to others according to the Golden Rule: Treat others as you wish to be treated. Living vicariously through others can broaden your horizons. Theirs is not your life, but you can appreciate the life others have. Don't be angry if someone has more than you do. What they have that you don't may be all in your mind. You may have something they lack, as well.

Once you have learned to forgive, it's time to move forward by accepting that what's done is done. Leave it in the past and plan for the future, and then put that plan into action. You may need to adjust those plans, as circumstances do change from time to time, but stay on the path toward success, and you will never fail. Stay positive and keep negative thoughts and influences out of your life.

Positive attitudes attract positive people, and those are the people you want in your life. When you surround yourself with positive people and energy, you can share and be open about what is going on in your life. Again, you have a support system to take you by your hand and guide you through the challenges. You will find there comes a mutual respect and a true love for newfound relationships, and you will begin to value others' words. True friendships don't harbor grudges, they don't judge, but they do forgive. That is the way life should be. If you want to develop good, close friendships, you need to be willing to open up your heart and mind.

At times when you don't know what to do and a new agenda seems hidden, turn to others. Help is always out there, and often times it only costs time. There are people who have been or who are going through exactly the same thing you are. Bring these people into your world and befriend them Use their successes and stories of different trials they used, and correlate them to your situation. Others can give you hope, and you will have faith that things will get better. These people will give you the strength to find joy, and very soon, your struggle will come to an end, and you will be in a far better place, no matter where that place is.

Having faith in something, whether it's faith in God, yourself, your determination, whatever it is, will see you through, but you must begin with baby steps or you will get frustrated and quit. Never stop hoping that things will get better. Keep that faith strong, keep those people close and you will soon find the success you seek. This is true with anything in life, not just with serious injury. Having hope, faith and love in your life will guide you to greatness

Yet, sometimes it does seem to be just too much to handle on your own. There may come a point in your recovery, or on your journey, when you need more help than family or friends can give. You may find yourself depressed; you may find you are just too weak on your own. There is no shame in seeking professional help to get you through the most difficult struggles. You may need to talk to a psychologist or counselor to help you get over that hurdle. That's okay. At some point, we all need that extra push, and a professional may be the one to offer you that extra help. Talking about obstacles and setbacks in your progress may give you a better understanding of how you can keep working toward your goal. Someone objective, detached from your situation, may be able to see what you don't. You may need that objectivity to see it for yourself. Talking it out often causes people to be enlightened, and they see what they need to do in order to keep moving forward, to keep from giving up. Once again, you must never give up. There is always a good outcome when you keep trying.

Certain ideas from others, short sayings that contain words of wisdom, can reinforce beliefs and attitudes, and some have helped me to stay focused.

One quote that I believe is true for everybody comes from Bill Cosby: "If you can find humor in anything, you can survive it." Humor can be found in anything and laughter often times aids in healing. Even at traditionally somber places, like funeral homes, recalling humorous memories may help those coping with a loss. If we can laugh with others and sometimes at ourselves, we can deal with any misfortune that life tosses our way. Joking around with my therapists eased the burden of being away from family and friends for such a long time.

Another quote that has meaning for me is "My past has brought me to where I am today and I wouldn't change a thing." If I had a chance to live my life over, oddly enough, I would choose to experience the accident again. That is not to say that I enjoyed all the work it took to get where I am today, nor do I enjoy the restrictions that accompany my injuries, but I would not be the person I am today without the difficult times. My faith tells me God has a plan for my life that included the car wreck. I want to say that I would not want to go through my ordeal again, but I accept my life as a gift from God.

Often times people associate losing with failure. Another quote that I like, "Failure is nothing more than the first step to success in your next step" shows an alternate view. For example, in junior high our basketball team did not win all their games in regular season, but the players were building skills and unity that led to a successful post season.

John W. Gardner, author of books on leadership, provided the following quote that I also can relate to: "Feeling sorry for yourself is a slippery slope and it impedes progress." When tragedy strikes, feeling sorry for yourself is a waste of time. That time could be spent in recovery. Feeling sorry for yourself often clouds your perspective, making you think others should be doing more for you. When others start doing more for you, you start doing less for yourself. You need to work hard and do as much as you can for yourself.

Inspirational quotes that relate to your situation can be found in a variety of places. Newspapers and magazines often contain words of wisdom. The internet can be another source, and whole books of quotations can be found in libraries and bookstores. Drugstores, gift shops, and card stores, any places that have gift sections, often have inspirational plaques that can be purchased to display where they will be seen often. Finding one or some that pertain to your life and displaying them in a prominent place may be an inspiration and daily reminder to keep your focus.

In conclusion, I thought that I had my life all planned out. The early education I had planned was leading me to the college which I selected. I was top of the game in sports, particularly, basketball. I was driven, determined, and nothing got in my way of achieving my goals. Then my life was turned on a black-ice dime. No longer shooting hoops and living an adventurous life (at least for a substantial niche of time,) I had to learn how to do the basic things that a toddler can do... all over again. Small steps, one after another, were taken that eventually led to where I wanted to be, where I am.

The person I am today has evolved because of obstacles, determination, and perseverance. Since the transplant my new kidney works excellently, after a few minor problems. It is no surprise that I still enjoy sports. I enjoy watching sports, attending nearby sporting events with friends and catching competitions on TV. I visit friends and relatives and play cards regularly with some acquaintances. Deficiencies in my balance and mobility limit my participation in team sports, so cards are a tool I use to fill my competitive spirit away from home.

I enjoy music. Modern country is my favorite, but I am known to sing Kenny Rogers "The Gambler" whenever I sing karaoke, any chance I get. I am atrocious at singing- I have been told I was bad before the accident and am worse now- but I still enjoy it. I also enjoy dancing, for example at weddings, but with lack of fluid movement, I am restricted to slow dancing.

At times I attend college or professional sporting events with family or friends. I have many pleasant and humorous memories from these events, but most of them probably are interesting only to those who experienced them with me. However, one thing that I would like to tell has to do with a Cincinnati Reds baseball game. On April 26, 2012, I was granted the opportunity to throw out a ceremonial first pitch for the Cincinnati Red's game played at Great American Ball Park. I was a pitcher in high school but remained skeptical about how I would throw from the mound at this time because my balance is nowhere near where it once was. I believe that pitching is 90% balance, but what fun would life be if there were no obstacles to conquer?

My time at Great American Ball Park was shared with four friends, Brian, Dan, Rodney, and Shelley. Shelley and her friend Jerry took pictures, and she put a video together. Pitching that day was an experience that I will never forget. I was amazed that still have the ability to throw the baseball with accuracy.

I regard family as the focal point in my life. I still feel that my Dad is the smartest person I know, and he is still my hero. He is everything that I want to be. It starts with his choice of mate. I cannot express how much Mom and Dad mean to me. My Dad and I still do many things together. We cut wood, tend the garden, care for the yard, and still throw ball or Frisbees around. I still see my cousins often, and on holidays, Super Bowl Sunday, or other special days, many of my aunts, uncles, and cousins in the area get together.

My sister now lives in Cincinnati and is married to a wonderful man; they have three boys. I am the godfather for all three of my nephews. Andrew is the big brother as he will start second grade in the fall, 2012. Younger brothers Grant and Nicholas will soon be following in Andrew's footsteps. I have the opportunity to see them often, but since they live just short of three hours away, our meetings aren't frequent enough. Although I'm single, I hope God brings a special lady into my life, at some point.

Regardless of it all, I still stay on the path of what I wanted to do all along – help others. I try motivating others by giving speeches at schools, churches, and organizations It turns out my view was right in the end. I do positively influence lives, not as a traditional teacher, but in many places not limited to the classroom. I hope that reading this book helps you in whatever area of your life that you want to change for the better, but my story can only help you so much.... THE REST IS UP TO YOU.

"Failure only increases your chances for success at your next attempt."

162

Taking the signs from the stretch at GABP
April 26, 2012

What Others Have to Say About Matt

Alan Unterbrink: Guidance Counselor, Delphos St. John High School : Matt randomly called me at school. He was requesting to speak to our student body. Matt explained the circumstances surrounding his accident. After much discussion, we decided to give him the opportunity to speak to our students. His intent was to speak motivationally and talk about making intelligent decisions. I could not believe how Matt was able to hold the attention of our students. He did a tremendous job of challenging the students to make appropriate choices and to make the most of their lives. Matt's talk was heartfelt, educational and interesting. I believe he made an enormous impression on many of our students. Matt's ability to physically overcome his accident is truly amazing. However, what impresses me even more is how upbeat he is about his present condition and how he looks forward to the rest of his life. He has accepted all challenges and conquered most. Matt has been a true inspiration to me. I am extremely honored to call him my friend.

Greg Pettit – Patrick Henry High School: Matt does a tremendous job of motivating all people to overcome their obstacles and realizing that the sky is, indeed, the limit. Matt's presentation held the attention of the audience and inspired them to "reach for the stars". Matt's use of humor and real life stories solidified his presentation and received nothing but great feedback from students and staff. I highly recommend Matt Schroeder for a presentation at your school.

Dick Kortokrax -- Kalida High School Boys Basketball: What a dynamic presentation Matt Schroeder gave to our players about how he was determined to prove his doctors wrong in that he was going to walk again. What an impacting message he had about how important it was for him to stay mentally sound and continue to have a strong determination in order to achieve a goal of this nature. To me, Mr. Schroeder has a powerful message to offer for boys and girls of any age in any walk of life on what it takes to achieve one's goal(s) in life!

Kerry Johnson, Principal – Pandora-Gilboa High School: On Thursday, December 4th, 2008, Mr. Matt Schroeder delivered a motivational presentation to our juniors and seniors here at Pandora-Gilboa High School. Matt's presentation grabbed the attention of our students and opened their eyes on how best to respond to adversity. His message is one that holds a great deal of value for high school kids. After the presentation, Matt invited written feedback from the students and the results were overwhelmingly positive. I recommend that you give strong consideration to having Matt deliver his message at your respective school.

Matt Schroeder